Nothing
Comes Easy

Y.A. Tittle with Kristine Setting Clark

TRIUMPH
BOOKS

Triumph Books and colophon are registered trademarks of Random House, Inc.

Library of Congress Cataloging-in-Publication Data

Tittle, Y. A. (Yelberton Abraham), 1926–
    Nothing comes easy / Y.A. Tittle with Kristine Setting Clark.
        p. cm.
    Includes bibliographical references.
    ISBN-13: 978-1-60078-210-7
    ISBN-10: 1-60078-210-8
    1. Tittle, Y. A. (Yelberton Abraham), 1926– 2. Football players—United States—Biography. I. Clark, Kristine Setting, 1950– II. Title.
    GV939.T5A26 2009
    796.332092--dc22
    [B]   2009022432

This book is available in quantity at special discounts for your group or organization. For further information, contact:

Triumph Books
542 South Dearborn Street
Suite 750
Chicago, Illinois 60605
(312) 939-3330
Fax (312) 663-3557
www.triumphbooks.com

Printed in U.S.A.
ISBN: 978-1-60078-210-7
Design by Sue Knopf
All photos courtesy of Y.A. Tittle unless otherwise indicated

Contents

vii **Foreword by Frank Gifford**

xv **Introduction by Steve Sabol**

First Quarter: Football—the Love of My Life

3 **Chapter 1** Marshall, Texas

11 **Chapter 2** The Mavericks

21 **Chapter 3** Myron Baylock, Mrs. Poole's Boarding House, and Red Swanson

27 **Chapter 4** 1944: The LSU Tigers

31 **Chapter 5** 1945: The T Formation

37 **Chapter 6** 1946: A Winning Season

39 **Chapter 7** 1947: The Belt-Buckle Game

43 **Chapter 8** 1948: The Year of the Quarterback

Second Quarter: The Colts, the 49ers, and the Giants

49 **Chapter 9** In the Blink of an Eye— from Cleveland to Baltimore

57 **Chapter 10** Baltimore: A Real Football Town

67 **Chapter 11** Cecil Isbell: The Man Who Taught Me How to Pass

73 **Chapter 12** The Disbanding of the Colts Franchise

81 **Chapter 13** The Flip of a Coin—from Baltimore to San Francisco

87   **Chapter 14** Quarterback Frankie Albert

93   **Chapter 15** I Came to San Francisco to Play

105 **Chapter 16** Hardy Brown: The Toughest Football Player
                 I Ever Met

113 **Chapter 17** A Quarterback Controversy

119 **Chapter 18** The Big Three: Shaw, Strader, and Albert

133 **Chapter 19** 1957: The Year of the Alley-Oop

141 **Chapter 20** A Changing of the Guard

145 **Chapter 21** The Beginning of the End

149 **Chapter 22** I'll Quit Before I Play in New York!

Third Quarter: The New York Giants, 1961 to 1964

159 **Chapter 23** The New Kid in Camp

163 **Chapter 24** The Trade for Del Shofner

167 **Chapter 25** Getting Ready for the Big Push

175 **Chapter 26** Sharing the Quarterback Position

179 **Chapter 27** The 1961 NFL Eastern Division Championship

185 **Chapter 28** Frank Gifford: The Comeback Kid

191 **Chapter 29** Beat the Packers!

195 **Chapter 30** Never Winning the Big One

199 **Chapter 31** The End of an Era

Fourth Quarter: Life after Football

205 **Chapter 32** Civilian Life

207 **Chapter 33** The Hall of Fame

209 **Chapter 34** Reflections

211 **Appendix I:** Tittle's Career, Season by Season

219 **Appendix II:** Team Schedules (Baltimore Colts 1948–1950, San
      Francisco 49ers 1951–1960, New York Giants 1961–1964)

229 **Appendix III:** Passing Statistics

231 **Sources**

Foreword

IT'S BEEN SAID THAT Y.A. TITTLE WAS ONE OF THE greatest quarterbacks to ever play the game. I am a testament to that statement.

It's been said that Y.A. Tittle was one of the greatest quarterbacks to ever play the game.

Y.A.'s coming to New York in August 1961 took courage. He was highly respected by players but had never been considered a star in San Francisco. When the 49ers decided to go with the shotgun offense, they also decided to go with a young quarterback out of Stanford University by the name of John Brodie.

Another well-known fact was that most quarterbacks who had started their pro football careers the same year as Y.A.—Johnny Lujack, Charley Trippi, and Harry Gilmer—had already succumbed to retirement.

When Y.A. joined the Giants, he walked into a very difficult situation. Charlie Conerly was the quarterback, and no one from the tightly knit offensive unit was going to become friendly with the man who might take his job. Why become a backup quarterback to an established and popular quarterback? Why inflict again the mental and physical punishment and the severe asthma attacks that made his special medication part of the team doctor's on-field equipment?

During practice with the New York Giants, Gifford catches a pass from Y.A.

Knowing Y.A. as I do now, his decision probably hung on his pride and the fact that if he retired, his family's last memories of his football days would be the difficult times in San Francisco.

The future looked bleak for the man we affectionately referred to as "Colonel Slick," but I knew that the professional athlete that I had watched, admired, and played against for so many years still had a lot of good football left in him.

In 1962 I returned to the New York Giants after a brief retirement. When I arrived Y.A. was the team's new quarterback, and the new coach—Allie Sherman—had switched me from halfback to flanker.

In the beginning my return to professional football was a nightmare. My biggest problem was getting in sync with Y.A. Some quarterbacks throw soft balls and some throw hard balls. Charlie Conerly threw such soft passes that I would catch them one-handed in practice. It was that easy. Y.A., on the other hand, had a cannon for an arm. He also had a sidearm delivery that gave his passes a unique trajectory, a ball that often came to you as a blur out of the line of scrimmage. In addition, I had to adjust to Y.A.'s timing. Charlie would toss the ball just as I made my break to the inside or outside. Y.A. would hold on to the ball a split second longer and then bang it to me after I made my break. Same accuracy but fractions of a second later and with a hell of a lot more velocity.

Though I dropped almost everything Y.A. threw me at first, I felt reasonably sure we'd eventually jell. But in the final exhibition game against Philadelphia—with my back killing me and my hamstring tight as a drum—I dropped three passes that were right in my hands. It was the perfect cap to my entire preseason. I felt mortified.

On opening day against the Browns in Cleveland, I found myself on the bench. Allie Sherman had picked up a player from San Francisco named Aaron Thomas to start as flanker. Needless to say, I was devastated. My career and my attempted comeback appeared to be over.

The following week the team flew to St. Louis to play the Cardinals. Since Aaron Thomas had hurt his knee the previous Sunday, I knew I might get a chance to play. Sure enough, Allie started me at flanker.

Y.A. and I had developed a great rhythm, and I owe so much of my success that season to him.

As we huddled up, Y.A. looked at me and asked, "Can you beat Fischer?"

He was referring to Pat Fischer, a tough little Cardinals cornerback who later became an All-Pro with the Redskins.

"Yeah," I replied, trying to sound very confident. "I can beat him deep."

"Beat him on the fly?" asked Y.A., arching his eyebrows.

I just nodded. So Y.A. called the play: "Strong right, split left, B circle. I'll need some time, guys. On three…break!"

At the snap, I took it straight up the field and gave Fischer a little move to the inside, as if I were going to take it over the middle. He bought it, and I blew right by him. But I was shocked how quickly he recovered, and he was right with me when Y.A. had to let it go. Seeing me covered, he just let it rip. Basically, Y.A. was throwing it away. I don't know how the hell I got there; I sure wasn't that fast. And when I left my feet, the ball was still way beyond me. As I dove for the ball, I literally caught the end of it. Somehow I pulled it in to me before turning sideways and crashing into the end zone. It was the luckiest catch I ever made, and I sensed everything was going to be okay from then on.

Not only did I start the rest of the season, averaging 20 yards a catch, but I went to the Pro Bowl in a third position—something no one had, or has, ever done. UPI named me NFL Comeback Player of the Year. It wasn't the MVP award, but considering how my comeback started, that honor struck me as near miraculous.

Y.A. and I had developed a great rhythm, and I owe so much of my success that season to him. He wanted his pass patterns run precisely the way they should be run—so many steps up field, the fake, the cut, the drive inside or out. We worked and worked on each pattern until we had it choreographed much like a ballet performance.

Y.A. would take the snap and sprint back, never backpedal, always the same number of steps, always the same number of yards, then plant that rear foot and fire the ball. It always arrived in the right place at the precise instant I came open. Y.A.'s passing routine was so exactly calibrated that, after about a half hour of practice, he'd have literally dug a hole with the right foot that he planted before the throw. Sometimes we'd have to move to a new spot on the field.

Our favorite pattern was the zig-out, and it became our bread-and-butter play against man-to-man coverage. My job was to drive to the cornerback and give it a hard move to the inside, looking back at Y.A. He would time his pump-fake to my inside move, and the cornerback had to commit. At that very instant, I'd plant my inside foot and break hard to the outside. I loved that play, and so did Y.A. We shortened a few careers with it over the three years we were together.

Tittle was a real superstitious character who insisted that we adhere to a culinary pregame routine. It started the Saturday night before the sixth game of the '62 season. We were staying at the Roosevelt Hotel near Grand Central Station, and late in the evening a bunch of us on the offense set out for a bite to eat. We walked and walked but found no restaurant open. Finally we landed in this ratty old Italian joint, literally a hole-in-the-wall. After checking the menu on the stained wall, Y.A. suggested that we all try the spaghetti and meatballs, and amazingly enough, they turned out to be marginally edible. The following day we launched an ulcer-risking nine-game winning streak.

For the next three years, on the night before every home game, Y.A. dragged us to that dump for spaghetti and meatballs. To this day, the mere thought of those reddish-brown mounds makes me queasy. But Y.A. loved to slop that stuff down almost as much as he believed it was helping us win. Nor, unfortunately, did he mind sacrificing our gastrointestinal systems to the cause.

Before the last game of the season, and the final game of both our careers, I found myself standing next to Y.A. on the steps of the Yankee Stadium dugout. He looked up at the December sky and said, "Frank, this is what I loved more than anything else. This one moment just before you go out on that field. No one could ever understand what this dadgummed stadium has meant to me." I knew exactly what he meant.

In 1964 both Y.A. and I retired from professional football. He had stood at the forefront of the Giants offense for four years and led the Giants to three straight Eastern Division titles—1961, 1962, and 1963. Besides his many gridiron achievements, Y.A. also holds the distinction of being the first quarterback—and one of only six in NFL history—to have achieved consecutive 30-touchdown passing seasons.

Y.A. was inducted into the Pro Football Hall of Fame in 1971. His presenter was Giants owner and dear friend Wellington

Mara, who, in 1977, would be my presenter. During Wellington's presentation of Y.A., he told the Canton audience
that "the glory years of the Giants [were]
when Tittle was at the helm."

As for the man I affectionately referred
to as "Colonel Slick," Y.A. Tittle will forever be remembered as one of the elite
to have donned the New York Giants
uniform.

—Frank Gifford

Introduction

Y.A. TITTLE PLAYED 17 SEASONS OF PROFESSIONAL FOOTBALL
and was the first quarterback selected to the Pro Football Hall of
Fame who never won a championship. He played three seasons
with the Baltimore Colts of the All-America Football Conference
(1947–1949) and one with the Colts in the National Football League
(1950). He played 10 seasons with the San Francisco 49ers and his
final four seasons with the New York Giants. Although Tittle had
excellent personal statistics while playing for the Colts and 49ers, the
one thing that continued to elude him was an NFL championship.

The championship was Tittle's "white whale." He chased it for
15 years with three teams through countless cities.
Like Captain Ahab he committed his body and soul
to its capture.

After a year with Baltimore, Tittle's championship
chase began in earnest with the San Francisco 49ers.

The championship was Tittle's "white whale."

Tittle would use anything and anybody that promised success.
With the 49ers he had an acrobatic receiver by the name of R.C.
Owens, and he developed a unique pass play called the Alley-Oop.

In his 10 years with the 49ers, Tittle won many games but
never a championship. In 1961, at the age of 34, he was traded to
the New York Giants.

In Tittle's first year with the Giants he led the league in touchdown passes, and in the last game of the season New York claimed
the Eastern Division title.

But in the championship game there were no tears of joy—only tears of sorrow as Tittle's Giants were crushed by Vince Lombardi's Packers, 37–0.

In 1962 Tittle led New York to another Eastern title, but in the championship game the brute power of the Packers again denied him the one victory he wanted most.

In 1963 a determined Y.A. Tittle set his sights once again on the NFL championship. Teams knew that Tittle was the Giants' strength, and they pressured him a great deal. The 1963 season best characterized Tittle's makeup and championship qualities—not only his expertise and his skills but the mentality and strength of this man.

For the third consecutive year Tittle directed the Giants to the Eastern Division title and he was named the league's MVP. But the hard season had taken its toll on Tittle. He was battered, injured, and weak, and the suspicion arose that he would not be able to play in the championship game against the Chicago Bears. But Tittle refused to let his knee injury keep him sidelined.

At Chicago's Wrigley Field, the Giants went after the NFL championship on a wing and a prayer. The wing was Tittle's arm; the prayer was for his legs. Tittle passed the Giants to an early lead, but in the second quarter he was hit by a blitzing linebacker—crumbling his legs beneath him.

The Bears battled back and went ahead 14–10. With time running out Y.A. Tittle, aging and aching after 16 years in pro football, continued in vain to pursue the one victory that had always eluded him.

Sometimes winning isn't everything. It's the will to win that is the only thing, and it carried Y.A. Tittle to the Pro Football Hall of Fame.

—*Steve Sabol*
President, NFL Films

Nothing
Comes Easy

First Quarter

Football—
the Love of My Life

1

Marshall, Texas

FOOTBALL HAS BEEN MY ENTIRE LIFE. My teachers used to say, "Y.A., if you don't quit looking out the window at those guys kicking the football you'll never amount to anything."

In hindsight, not only do I disagree with them but I see football as the catalyst for my life's successes.

Any boy who grew up in the town of Marshall during the 1930s was destined to play football. Marshall wasn't exactly what one would call a "swinging" town. It was during the time of the Great Depression, and both money and amusement were at an all-time low. As for me personally, it didn't really matter, because all I wanted to do was play football.

Football has been my entire life.

Putting the ball in the air was the way I learned to play the game, and I have believed and lived up to that motto ever since. Football is all about passing, and passing is what I do best. Give me a choice to run or throw the ball, and I will choose the latter every time. In order to win you must score points, and the fastest and easiest way to score is by putting the ball in the air.

One of my neighbors was future Hall of Fame member Sammy Baugh. At that time he was an All-American quarterback at Texas Christian University. Every kid on our scrub teams wanted to be like Slingin' Sammy. We would all argue as to who would play the quarterback position. The kids in Marshall not only idolized Sammy, but his style of play was emulated by each and every one of us.

From every backyard tree hung an old tire. All of us spent countless hours throwing footballs through the loops as we had seen Baugh do in the old newsreels. The guy who could thread the needle most often was granted the esteemed quarterback position for that day's football game. We all dreamed of someday being as great as Sammy Baugh.

I consider myself to be a little more fortunate than many of my friends. My oldest brother, Jack, seven years my senior, introduced me to the game of football. While I was still attending elementary school, Jack was a gridiron star at Marshall High School. He is the one responsible for teaching me how to hold the ball and how to throw it. He tried teaching me other aspects of the game, but I somehow always got back to the subject of passing.

He told me that it was important that I learn the rest of the game, too. I knew he was right, but first and foremost I wanted to be a quarterback. Whenever I told him that, Jack would become enraged and throw up his hands in total disgust, but after calming down he would continue to work with me on becoming a better passer.

Jack was not only my brother; he was also my inspiration to be the best athlete that I could be. He was the town's football hero, and my secret ambition was to be as good—if not better—than he was. Like most brothers, there was a personal rivalry between us, a fierce competition that would never allow me to give up on trying to whip him—whether it was at football, marbles, or wrestling. It didn't matter; if it was competitive, I wanted to win.

When Jack beat me—and he usually did—I would keep him out in the backyard until I got even. When all else failed, I would try to wear him down. I have always hated losing, and over the years that has remained one of the constants in my life.

Once my brother had shown me the fundamentals of the game, I set out of find a receiver that I could practice with. My younger brother, Don, was the perfect match. At six years old and three years my junior, I was able to convince him that running was the most important aspect of the game.

"That's what coaches look for," I told him. "You've got to get your legs in shape and practice running if you want to make the football team."

Of course, he believed me—never suspecting that there were ulterior motives on my part.

"Well, as long as you are going to run, you might as well catch passes for me."

He was more than eager to do so.

I ran Don ragged and told him that a guy who complains never gets anywhere.

"The dedicated football players accept physical punishment as part of the game," I told him. He never once complained. He would rather have died than given up. In the long run it helped us both to become better football players.

As I mentioned before, Jack was an outstanding football player at Marshall High School and later at Tulane University, where he was a 205-pound blocking back in the single-wing formation. Don, who followed both Jack and me, was actually the best athlete of us all but lost interest in the game after playing in high school. I sometimes wonder if I burned him out by running him so much when we were kids.

In the beginning my father, a postman in the rural sections of Marshall, was opposed to having his boys play football. Yelberton Abraham Sr. was born in Sulphur Springs, Texas. Located in north Texas, the town's population was 8,000. In the early 1900s my father was a young man and worked very hard. There were more important things to do than become involved in something as trivial as sports.

When Jack told our parents that he wanted to go out for football at Marshall Junior High School, both my dad and mom objected—but for different reasons. Jack wasn't surprised when my dad objected because of his strict work ethic, but my mom, Alma, thought that football was too rough of a sport and was afraid her son would get hurt.

> *In the beginning my father, a postman in the rural sections of Marshall, was opposed to having his boys play football.*

Jack never gave up his desire to play. In fact he was so adamant about playing that my mom and dad finally broke down and gave him permission. My father was very strong-willed, but he was also fair. As with all generations, he realized that times had changed since his day as a young man.

In the beginning Jack's love for football really didn't interest my parents. Even though they had agreed to let him play, they were not completely sold on the idea. But things began to change when the people of Marshall began stopping my father on his mail route to ask him how his son was doing in football. Some would even praise Jack for the fine player that he was.

My father's pride in Jack as a great player transformed him into a pretty big football fan. I figured that my brother's success as a gridiron great would make me an automatic shoo-in when it came to my needing parental permission to play football for Marshall Junior High. I couldn't have been more wrong.

As a child I had suffered from bronchial asthma, and my folks were afraid to allow me to play such a rough game. Like my brother Jack, I too had to persuade them to let me try out. I can still remember my mother's reaction when she overheard me asking my father about football.

"Certainly not!" she said.

But with Jack on my side, the two of us eventually wore them both down, and they finally agreed to let me play. That was my first experience with the old double-team.

The asthma troubled me throughout high school. There were times on the field that I could barely breathe, but I never let on about my condition. I was afraid they would make me quit.

Jack's own football career contributed to my goal of surpassing his gridiron achievements. I always tried to top whatever he had accomplished. Even though I didn't always succeed, it forced me to compete at a higher level. Don't get me wrong, now. I was very proud of my brother's accomplishments. I just wanted to be as good of an athlete as Jack—or better.

My father inspired me in a different way. His inspiration didn't come from his athletic background, for he wasn't an athlete. It came from the fact that he was a good person.

My dad was a simple, kind, and good man. His first and only love was his family. He worked hard every day of his life to give his three boys and my sister Huline the best he could afford. You wouldn't call our family rich, but we were well fixed. We lived in a large brick home on 10 acres of land located approximately three miles outside of town. My parents had some cows, pigs, and chickens and a garden that supplied our family with vegetables.

We owned two cars and had a few dollars in the Marshall bank. We never were in want of anything.

Most of all our family had a great deal of love for one another—the kind of love that I have passed on to my own wife and children.

My dad was very proud of his boys and wasn't afraid to show it. One day my dad and I went into town to buy me a pair of shoes. When we walked into the store, my dad stuck out his chest, put his arm around my shoulder, and said to the salesman, "Come on, now. I want you to get my big football-playing boy a pair of those shoes over there."

Just then everyone in the store began to look around—possibly thinking that they would see Sammy Baugh or some other great football star.

Just then everyone in the store began to look around—possibly thinking that they would see Sammy Baugh or some other great football star. I was a little embarrassed, but that was the way my father was. His boys meant everything to him.

As they say in Texas, my dad was quite a "doer." Upon finishing his daily mail route, he would work on buildings and/or remodel the homes and stores around Marshall. If I remember correctly, he owned two or three pressing stores, a couple of coffee and sandwich shops, and some houses. My dad was an extremely hard worker whose main objective was to provide for his family.

I sometimes feel a little guilty that I didn't help more when it came to doing my share of the chores. But my burning desire to play football was more important to me than anything, and I'm sure my dad let me get away without doing those everyday tasks more times than not.

In 1949 my father passed away. It always pleased me that he lived long enough to see Jack play for Tulane and me play for

Louisiana State. He even got the chance to see me play when I was with the Baltimore Colts. It made me feel good to know that his sacrifices were not in vain. All my hard work learning to play football had finally paid off.

I wish I could say the same about my mom, but she passed in 1945 after the completion of my freshman year at LSU. She had become quite a fan of the game.

My dad taught me many important lessons about life, but there is one that particularly stands out: "No matter what you do, do the best you can." This is the approach I have taken with the game of football—study hard, practice hard, and play hard.

Aside from my family, football has been my greatest passion in life. Beginning in fourth grade, I organized a team and we whipped the fifth graders. I guess you could say that I was the promoter, the coach, and, of course, the quarterback. It was the beginning of a tremendous career in football, and even back then there was nothing better than putting the ball in the air.

2

The Mavericks

I WAS IN THE SIXTH GRADE WHEN I FOUND OUT that I could throw a football better than any other kid in Marshall. Unfortunately for me, though, the Marshall High School Junior Mavericks were not a passing team. Our coach, Joe Magrill, still believed that the best way to move the ball was to utilize the single-wing formation for both running and blocking. Despite the fact that we had different views on how to play the game, I still considered Joe to be a fine coach.

Coach Magrill was my brother Jack's coach. He spoke highly of my brother, and when I came out for the team at Marshall Junior High School, I was presented with Jack's old shoulder pads. There even was a ceremony for the presentation of the pads! This was a great moment in my early career, and I was proud to wear my brother's equipment.

When I first used the pads, I found them to be too big for me. I had trouble throwing in them, but since the Junior Mavericks were a running team, it really didn't matter. Actually Coach Magrill converted me to the tailback position in the double-wing, and I soon learned that there was much more to the game of football than just passing.

Throughout my first year I was a substitute player and didn't see much action. When I did have a chance to play, I rarely did anything that was worth talking about, but my desire to play must have impressed Coach Magrill. One day I overheard him tell my math teacher, "You watch ol' Y.A.; he's going to be better than his brother Jack."

Why he would say that was a curiosity to me. I never felt that I had accomplished that much on the football field. Still, it made me feel good to know he thought that much of me.

In 1938 most of my football was played on the sandlots and fields of Marshall. On the way home from school we would choose up sides and play tackle—no pads, no protection. At first my parents were worried that I would get hurt, but over time they got used to the fact that bumps and bruises were a part of the game. Back then parents didn't baby their children like the parents of today. As kids, we took care of ourselves and learned to shake off our gridiron injuries. If you couldn't do that, then you had no business playing the game of football.

The parents of today are far too protective of their children, but I must admit I, too, am guilty of that same crime. When my boys Mike and Pat were playing tackle football in the lot next to our home, I was so worried that they would get hurt. It seems almost hypocritical that a professional football player would worry about his boys playing tackle, but I did.

> *The parents of today are far too protective of their children, but I must admit I, too, am guilty of that same crime.*

In the town of Marshall you were either a football player or a football fan. Football was the *only* recreation in town, and as far as I know, it still is to this day.

Marshall was your typical small town centered around its two Marshall High football teams. On Friday nights Marshall Stadium would host a capacity crowd of 8,000 fans. Before the game there would be a parade. Stores would close down and schools would release their students early.

Back then, small towns not only kept track of their own teams but also of rival teams from other parts of the state. Marshall's rivalries included Longview, Kilgore, Gladewater, and Tyler. We had some great games against them. Even a few of the teams from the junior high school level became rivals. One team from Roberts Junior High School had a guy who played both center and fullback. His name was Bill Johnson. I played against him in my very first football game. Bill and I would end up on opposite sides of the line of scrimmage throughout junior high school, high school, and beyond. When I was quarterbacking for LSU, Bill played for Texas A&M. We shared some great games together. In the pros Bill played for the San Francisco 49ers in the All-America Conference and I was drafted by the Baltimore Colts. For the next three seasons we continued our gridiron rivalry. We had become very good friends over the years and became even closer when I joined the 49ers. By that time Bill had become one of my coaches.

When I returned for my second year of football at Marshall Junior High, Joe Magrill was still the coach. He still strongly believed in the single-wing formation, and I continued to see little action as a forward passer.

With the utilization of a running offense and me on the bench, Coach Magrill decided to try me out as a cornerback on defense. To my own surprise, I discovered that I really enjoyed driving my shoulder into a ball carrier and knocking him down. It was an incredible rush, but my desire to be a passing quarterback was still my first love.

By the time I had reached my third year of junior high football I was six feet tall and weighed 145 pounds. Robert "Cracker"

Brown had replaced Coach Magrill. I was elated that Coach Brown had taken over the helm, because he believed in throwing the football. This quality alone was enough for me. He continued to use the single-wing formation (the T had yet to be invented) and utilized me as a tailback with instructions to throw the ball whenever I got the chance.

Coach Brown allowed me to play "my" game. I threw the ball consistently, and the media built me up as a hotshot passer. One of the papers compared me to Sammy Baugh and said that I was just as good as he was in high school. I considered that statement to be the ultimate compliment.

Even with my artistic flair as a passer, the Junior Mavericks lost quite a few games that season. I began to question if passing was really the way to win football games.

My first year at Marshall High School was 1941. It was also the first year for our new football coach, Otis Mitchell. He brought a new attitude to Marshall—a winning attitude. Before he arrived, Marshall had spent many years as the league's doormat. Things were about to change, and this man from Pampa, Texas, would become extremely influential to my gridiron career.

I will never forget the first time I met Otis Mitchell. The varsity team was practicing on the field across from the high school when Coach Mitchell walked out on the field, blew his whistle, and brought the squad together. At first he just stood there reviewing his troops as if he were trying to analyze the gridiron talent he would or would not be blessed with. He then introduced himself and immediately ingrained his philosophy into our team.

"Gentlemen, my name is Otis Mitchell. I am your new coach. I think it will be better for all of us if I tell you right now that I have not come to Marshall to coach a losing football team. There is no such thing as a good loser. I do not want good losers on my football team!"

This was a totally different philosophy than what we had been raised on in the past. We were all brought up to believe that you showed good sportsmanship at all times and *especially* after experiencing a loss. Coach Mitchell saw it differently.

"If any of you are satisfied to finish second, then turn in your uniforms right now. I am looking for boys who want to win it all. The world is full of good losers. I want good winners!"

I have always wanted to win, and the words that Coach Mitchell articulated to the team that day stayed with me forever. Since that day, I never stepped on to the gridiron without hearing him say, "The world is full of good losers."

Mitchell's aggressive approach to winning carried over to his players. As a team we felt that it was only a matter of time until his winning philosophy would become a reality.

Physical training and conditioning were also an intricate part of Coach's beliefs, but when it came to mental preparation, he felt that the player must take responsibility in disciplining himself.

Coach Mitchell told the team, "Discipline is necessary in football. A player must discipline himself; he must follow the rules and train himself to live by them."

I followed his philosophy throughout my football career. I know there is a price that must be paid for playing this game, and believe me, I paid it. But more than anything else, I wanted to win, and in order to do so, I had to be willing to pay the price.

I have always wanted to win, and the words that Coach Mitchell articulated to the team that day stayed with me forever.

Back in those days some of my teammates smoked. I was not one of them. Football was tough enough without putting all that

15

smoke and toxins in your system. I wanted to give myself the best chance at winning.

Throughout my career I have seen athletes who could cast aside both the rules of physical training and psychological discipline and *still* play great. They have always amazed me with their skills. But for myself, I felt that I needed to take advantage of each and every opportunity. I found out that the best way to achieve this was to follow a set of rules to the letter. Then if I lost, I knew I didn't lose because I cut corners.

Another strong belief of Coach Mitchell's was to practice like you play. You practice as hard as you would if you were playing a game. He was right. I never wanted to let up for a second, and I never felt right about missing a practice due to a minor injury.

Coach Mitchell may have been a taskmaster, but he also made football a lot of fun. We threw the ball around a lot during practice. I enjoyed that immensely. Practices were part conditioning and part body contact. That gave a balance to our practice sessions. I never really felt exhausted after a workout, but then who does when you are 15 or 16 years old? You feel like you could go forever. As a matter of fact, there were times on Friday afternoons when we would play touch tackle for a couple of hours after school and then pile into my father's car and drive back to Marshall Stadium to play a game that same night.

I have only been overweight one time in my entire football career, and that one time was my first year in high school under Coach Mitchell. My father always felt that it would be better if I put on some weight before going out for the varsity team. He warned me, "At 145 pounds, they will run right over you! You have got to be bigger, Y.A.!"

He immediately devised a diet of eggnog and milk. Upon returning home each day from school my mother would pour me a couple of eggnogs followed by a quart-of-milk chaser. Sometimes my stomach would feel like it was going to explode right there at the kitchen table. When I reported to spring practice my teammates were in awe of my size and expressed as much. Nicknames such as "Fatty" and "Lard Butt" were heard within the huddle and on the sideline. Even though my weight had escalated to a whopping 175 pounds, I still had a good arm and could throw the ball effectively. But the extra pounds diminished my running ability.

Despite that fact, Coach Mitchell continued to utilize me in the double-wing position as a fullback and halfback. In one game I even played end. Through no fault of my own, I was named the Marshall Mavericks' Most Valuable Player.

The MVP trophy was awarded by the Sullivan Funeral Home in downtown Marshall. I was a little embarrassed to receive the award because my sister, Huline, who was my biggest fan, was the secretary for George and Bill Sullivan, who ran the funeral parlor.

As I was handed the trophy at our annual football dinner, I could just hear everyone saying, "How do you like that? Huline Tittle works for the Sullivan Funeral Home and Y.A. wins the trophy!"

I'm sure Huline didn't do anything illegal to help me win the honor. I am just as certain, however, that her pride and enthusiasm for her brother and football in general helped the Sullivans make their final choice.

The award may have come too soon, as the Mavericks did not have as good a season as did their supposed MVP.

My senior year was 1943. Coach Mitchell turned his boys into one of the best high school football teams in east Texas. We were victorious in every game in District Two. It was also payback time for many of our rivals, such as Tyler, Kilgore, Longview,

Gladewater, and Texarkana. We lost to Lufkin in the state championship, but we had a hell of a year.

I want to emphasize that in 1943 I was blessed with what was to be the fastest high school backfield in Texas history. In Coach Mitchell's double-wing offense, I played the tailback position. My three other backs were Byron Gillroy, Bobby Furth, and Billy Dinkle. They were all lightning fast and placed first, second, and third in the district in the 100-yard dash. They may not have been as fast as today's runners, but they all ran the 100 in less than 10 seconds, which was an extremely fast time in those days.

> *I want to emphasize that in 1943 I was blessed with what was to be the fastest high school backfield in Texas history.*

This '43 squad also produced two of the fastest ends in the state—Roy Moore and James Taylor. The combination of Gillroy, Furth, Dinkle, Moore, and Taylor gave me five great receivers to throw the ball to, and all of them had no trouble going the distance.

Marshall passed the ball more that year than any other school in the state. I personally threw the ball 15 or 20 times per game. Also, Coach didn't believe in playing conservatively. We threw from our own end zone, from our own 10-yard line, on first down and on fourth down. That kept the game exciting. As usual, when I threw the ball there was always one of my five ends there to catch it. I was completing 18 to 20 passes per game. It was great.

We did not throw long. I would hit my fast wingbacks in the flat with short, quick passes. They were all so fast that once they were out in the open, they were gone. No one could catch them.

I missed the last two games of the '43 season due to a knee injury. We were playing Longview, and Furth moved into my tailback position and won the game for us. The following week we defeated Tyler and once again earned a playoff berth against Lufkin in the state championship game.

Throughout my years at Marshall, it was Lufkin that always dominated. In those days schools were assigned to districts on the basis of total enrollment. Lufkin pulled in kids from all over the county, which in turn allowed them to become a powerhouse in Texas football. Their 1943 team was no exception.

Even though my leg was still in a wire splint, I pleaded with Coach Mitchell to let me play.

"It's my last chance—my last shot at these guys. I just have to play!"

Knowing how much this game meant to me, and against his better judgment, Coach agreed to let me play.

I ended up playing the entire game against Lufkin. I would take the snap from center, throw the pass, and then get knocked down. With the wire splint on my leg, I had trouble getting up. Gilroy and Furth would prop me up each time, and I would continue to throw the ball off one leg. We ended up losing the game 19–7.

In hindsight maybe I shouldn't have played in that game, but when you are a 15-year-old quarterback playing in a championship football game, it's pretty hard to not play.

My entire life I have always wanted to play every minute of every game, but I have never criticized or second-guessed a coach for not playing me. In my opinion the coach has to call the shots as he sees fit. Coach Mitchell taught me patience and the value of concealing my frustrations and anger—something that I would carry with me all the way to the professional level.

My entire life I have always wanted to play every minute of every game.

3

Myron Baylock, Mrs. Poole's Boarding House, and Red Swanson

IN JUNE 1944 I GRADUATED FROM MARSHALL HIGH SCHOOL. I had received many offers from a number of southwest colleges that were interested in recruiting me for their football teams. Their interest was based on two factors. First of all, I weighed 185 pounds and could throw the hell out of the ball, and second, due to my continued asthmatic condition I would most likely qualify as a 4-F in the draft.

The United States was still a year away from winning World War II, and with the lack of male athletes in the college ranks, my draft status was more important to the collegiate recruiters than my passing records. They also knew that regardless of how well I performed, they would have me for the full four years.

I received scholarship offers from five Texas institutions—TCU, Texas A&M, University of Texas, Rice, and Southern Methodist. I received one offer from Tulsa, Oklahoma, and two from Louisiana—one for Tulane, where my brother Jack had played, and the other from Louisiana State University (LSU). Many of these offers came in the form of a letter or phone call, and some schools sent a recruiter to my home.

These recruiters arrived at my parents' house bearing information about their school. They would stay for dinner and promote all the wonderful things they could do for me if I chose their college. My parents loved it and were very impressed that so many people were interested in their boy.

For me personally, I wasn't really that interested. I knew that I wanted to play college football but never really thought much about which college I would like to play for.

In 1944 the style of collegiate football recruiting completely lacked the strict regulations that exist today. Any college could invite any scholarship candidate to come and visit their campus. Most of my college visits were to Texas and Louisiana schools. I made several visits to Louisiana State and was particularly impressed with their head coach, Bernie Moore. I got to know him quite well and in time knew he would be the man I wanted to play for. In mid-May, a few weeks before I was to graduate from Marshall, I signed to play with LSU. My scholarship included tuition, books, and room and board, which was pretty standard for the time.

I knew that I wanted to play college football but never really thought much about which college I would like to play for.

The main reason I went with LSU was because of Bernie Moore, but my decision was also influenced by the fact that Louisiana State was one of the few all-civilian schools in the southwest. Throughout most of the war, many of the colleges had service programs, which meant that the guys playing football were older and more experienced. My competition at LSU would be against other 17-year-old players.

Three days before reporting to LSU I did something really stupid, something that only an immature 17-year-old boy would do. I traveled to Austin, Texas, to visit the University of Texas at the request of Myron Baylock, a UT recruiter. Everything happened so quickly that to this day I do not know what made me change my mind. The shame of violating my written and spoken agreement with Bernie Moore has been with me ever since. It happened a long time ago, but it still weighs heavily on my conscience.

Anyway, there I was in a car with a couple of assistant coaches from Texas heading for Austin on a scorching-hot June afternoon. At that time I was not yet fully aware what was happening, but apparently it had all been meticulously planned out well in advance. The plan was to enroll me in UT summer school, get me a part-time job and keep me hidden from LSU until fall practice was under way.

That evening we arrived in Austin. I was escorted to a large home close to the UT campus. The sign over the door said *Mrs. Poole's Boarding House.*

Mrs. Poole greeted me at the door, then quickly whisked me away to the front room where she had me sign the register and then showed me to my room. I can remember her words: "It's nice and quiet here. You'll like it at the university."

I unpacked my things and stepped out of my room. I noticed that the door next to my room was open. I leaned in and said, "Hiya, my name is Y.A. Tittle."

There was a blond, stocky guy lying on the bed. He rolled over on his side, looked at me for a second out of half-closed eyes, and said, "Glad to meet you. My name is Layne…Bobby Layne."

Layne didn't know who I was, but I sure knew who he was. He was a star at Highland Park High School in Dallas. He was a first-team All-State quarterback. It was said that he was the hottest quarterback in the entire state of Texas.

"They got you too, huh?" said Bobby. "Man, they don't miss anybody." Then he laughed.

Layne didn't know who I was, but I sure knew who he was.

Bobby and I were close in age, but he had an air about him that made him seem much older and more confident. I liked him a lot, but there was something about him that made me feel uncomfortable.

That evening I contemplated my situation. Competing with a first-team All-State quarterback would be difficult for me in making the team, but I wasn't going to let Bobby deflate my confidence. He would still have to prove that he could throw a better ball than I could. I was sure he couldn't. I held on to my confidence in my ability as a passer.

The following morning Blair Cherry took me to the C and S Sporting Goods store that was across the street from Mrs. Poole's. A guy by the name of Rooster Andrews ran the store and hired me to work two or three hours a day stacking boxes, sweeping, and running errands.

Blair Cherry had done the same for many of the other football players—all except Bobby Layne. He didn't have to do any menial work as the others did. He was a terrific baseball pitcher and had signed with a semipro team that had a franchise in Austin. They paid him extremely well. Bobby just seemed to be heads above us all when it came to smarts.

Even though Bobby was a big city slicker from Dallas and I was just a green kid from Marshall, we still had football in common—and that's all we needed to become good friends.

Another thing we both had in common was our intense drive to compete. In the evenings we would take off our shoes and race each other in the street in front of Mrs. Poole's establishment. Everyone thought we were crazy, but we loved the competition. We actually thrived on it.

When I used to run into Bobby during our professional football days, we'd sit down to have a few beers, and at some point the topic of conversation would always revert back to our days at Mrs. Poole's. Bobby would always comment on how many times he had outrun me during our barefoot races, and I would always respond with, "Like hell you did!" The reality is that I whipped him more than he did me. But I guess since neither one of us ever received awards for our running ability in the NFL, it really didn't matter who won.

Within a few weeks of arriving at Mrs. Poole's, I was ready to go home. I regretted the fact that I had ever gone there in the first place. The guys were just different than what I was used to and had grown up with in Marshall.

About this same time, my mother had put in a call to Bernie Moore at LSU. She told him that I wasn't happy in Austin and was sure that I would be much happier at Louisiana State.

Bernie immediately contacted his line coach, Red Swanson, and told him to go to Austin and find me. He had strict orders "not to return without Y.A."

Bright and early the following Sunday morning, Red showed up at Mrs. Poole's. I met him in the hotel for breakfast. It never occurred to me as to why he was there. It was immediately obvious to him that I was unhappy at Austin, so he asked me if I would reconsider and come to LSU. I couldn't wait to pack my bags, but first there was something that Red wanted me to do. He wanted me to call Dana X. Bible, the head football coach at Texas and tell him that I had changed my mind about playing at UT.

The thought of calling Coach Bible scared me to death. I tried everything I could think of to get out of making that call, but it seemed that Red was one step ahead of me. He knew that Coach wouldn't be in his office because it was Sunday; therefore, he went to the trouble of looking up Coach's home phone number.

The thought of calling Coach Bible scared me to death.

I felt trapped. I copied down the number and slowly walked over to a nearby phone booth. My heart was in my throat. I dialed the number and let it ring three or four times. To my relief, no one was at home.

Due to Red's respect and consideration of others, the University of Texas was at least given the opportunity to know that I was leaving, which is far more than the Texas coaching staff afforded the coaches of LSU when they talked me out of going to Louisiana State.

Red escorted me back to Mrs. Poole's, where I packed my suitcase and left. No one had even known that I had gone—not even Bobby Layne.

On the way to Baton Rouge, Swanson stopped in Houston to pick up another football player by the name of Jim Cason. Little did I know that we would become very good friends in the years to come. Jim and I played together at LSU for four seasons and later as teammates with the San Francisco 49ers. Jim was only 16 at the time, and believe me, we were both pretty scared. Most of the trip was spent in silence—he looking out one window, and I looking out the other.

I have often wondered what would have happened if I had stayed at Texas in the summer of '44. Maybe pro football would never have heard of me, or perhaps Bobby Layne's career would have been altered. Maybe we would have eliminated each other with our competitiveness—who knows?

Fate seems to have a way of changing things, and my fate was Red Swanson. He brought me to LSU and changed my life forever. Although my path and Bobby's path would cross many times over the next 20 years, I strongly believe that this was how it was meant to be.

4

1944: The LSU Tigers

JIMMY AND I ARRIVED IN BATON ROUGE JUST IN TIME TO BEGIN summer practice. From the beginning I knew that things would be much better at Louisiana State.

Most of the guys were my age, and the team was basically made up of freshmen and 4-Fs. I didn't have to compete against the older, more experienced guys like I would have if I had stayed in Austin.

Don't get me wrong, though; there was definitely no shortage of talent at LSU in 1944. Besides Jim Cason and myself, there was Red Knight from Bossier City, Louisiana, who was a top runner and kicker and Ray Coates from Jesuit High School in New Orleans who was the finest high school tailback in the state. He was a good runner and a fairly good passer who knew how to scramble for yardage when he had to.

Actually, Coach Moore was grooming Coates as the No. 1 tailback when I arrived in June. I may not have been a good runner or, for that matter, even a fair one, but when it came to passing I was the best on the team.

Bernie Moore would later call his '41 team "the finest backfield I ever coached." But in June 1944 we were nothing more than a ragamuffin team that needed a great deal of coaching, because underneath all that scruff and energy was a great deal of talent that only Coach Moore could bring to the surface.

Practices at LSU were quite different than what I was used to. We had double practices every day, one in the afternoon—where the temperature rose to over 100 degrees—and one at night. It was really tough. There was no time for anything but football and academics, and at times our studies took a backseat to the demands of the gridiron. By the end of summer practice I had dropped 10 pounds, but I was in the best shape of my life and ready to take on the competition.

We had double practices every day, one in the afternoon—where the temperature rose to over 100 degrees—and one at night.

The time had come for our first big intrasquad game, and Cason, Coates, Knight, and I were now the best of the tailback candidates. We all got a chance to play during that game, and I had a great night completing my first 12 passes and taking the offense down the field for two scores.

I guess I made a good impression on the media, because the following day the papers gave me a lot of print—a lot of good print. They said I might be the best passer to play for LSU since Leo Byrd and Able Michael. Naturally I was honored to even be mentioned in the same breath as those guys.

But collegiate football in the 1940s was not a passing game. Bernie Moore kept reiterating that "there is more to football than just throwing the ball." I knew he was right, but passing was all I knew how to do.

The 1944 season would not be noted as an outstanding one for Bernie Moore and his Tigers. Even though I got to start in four of our eight games, our overall record was 2–5–1 and our conference record was 2–3–1. Our only wins were against Georgia (15–7) and Tulane (25–6). We tied Alabama 27–27.

The two games that stand out most in my mind that year are our opener with Alabama and our last game of the season against Tulane.

Alabama was led by the great passer, Harry Gilmer. LSU was far from favored in this game, but I was more interested in competing against Gilmer than I was in the odds. Back then he was called "the finest forward passer in the nation," and I was eager to see just how good he really was. Gilmer turned out to be everything they said he was. Not only could he pass, but he could run—something I wasn't very good at. But that night I was right on target as we held Alabama to a 27–27 tie, which was one of the major upsets of the year in collegiate football.

My most outstanding game as a freshman, and maybe even my entire college career, was when we played Tulane in the season closer. Tulane was my brother Jack's school and was a bigger and tougher ballclub comprised of many servicemen, many of whom had played with Jack three years before. That day I completed 15 of 17 passes for three touchdowns and 300 yards as we annihilated the Green Wave 25–6.

Even though it would be many years before the passing game would encompass college football, I was given my one day in the sun to change all that. Coach Moore gave me the okay to put the ball in the air, and I did. Fewer games have given me greater satisfaction.

That day my mom, dad, and sister Huline drove 250 miles from Marshall just to see me play Tulane. My brother Jack was also in the stands. I knew he was proud of my performance, but I'm sure his pride was hurt having his alma mater whipped by an underrated LSU team with an all-freshmen backfield.

That day I completed 15 of 17 passes for three touchdowns and 300 yards as we annihilated the Green Wave 25–6.

As far as academic achievements go, my freshman year proved to be even less impressive than our football season. I think the main reason for that had to do with the war—with the draft. Everyone who attended college was just biding their time until their number came up for the draft. Even though I had asthma, I still expected to be drafted along with the others. I honestly didn't feel that this would qualify as a 4-F condition. As a result, I didn't take my studies very seriously, and if Coach Moore hadn't made me go to summer school that year, I would have been ineligible to play football my sophomore year at LSU.

In the spring of 1944, Uncle Sam sent me a letter that began with "Greetings." I had been called upon to report for my physical. The army classified me as 4-F. At first I was extremely embarrassed of my classification. The stereotypical 4-F candidate was considered to be scrawny and meek with horn-rimmed glasses and fallen arches. I certainly did not want to be associated with that! I felt better, though, when Cason, Coates, and Knight also qualified for the 4-F status.

5

1945: The T Formation

1945 WAS THE YEAR OF THE T FORMATION AT LOUISIANA STATE, and it changed my life forever as a passer. My teammates and I had heard a lot about this "new" formation but had never seen it demonstrated. That was to change the day Bernie Moore showed up at practice and introduced us to a guy by the name of Carl Brumbaugh.

Brumbaugh utilized the T formation when he played quarterback for the Chicago Bears back in the 1930s. But the strategy of the T took a backseat for a while to make room for the single- and double-wing formations—that is until Bears owner George Halas resurrected it in the 1940s. As a matter of fact, it was in December 1940 when Halas' Bears annihilated the Washington Redskins 73–0 by using the T formation in the NFL Championship Game.

Coach Halas summoned two of the smartest college coaches in football—Ralph Jones from Delaware College and Clark Shaughnessy from the University of Chicago—to come to the Bears training camp to redesign the T formation for his club. Shaughnessy and Jones together changed the T by adding a man in motion and a counterplay while giving the formation a sense of deception and speed. After the Bears' memorable rout of Washington, the T formation was utilized in both college and pro ball.

In 1941 Shaughnessy left Halas to take on the head coaching position at Stanford. With help from quarterback Frankie Albert and fullback Norm Standlee, his ballclub went undefeated that year (his first year as coach) and gained a berth in the Rose Bowl, where they beat Nebraska 21–13.

If I remember correctly, the first Southwestern Conference team to switch to the T formation from the single- and double-wing formations was Rice University, followed by Georgia and then Louisiana State.

When Coach Moore hired Brumbaugh to come to LSU he sent two of his assistants to South Bend, where Notre Dame was also changing over to the T. Bernie's intentions were to learn as much about the formation as possible in as short a time as possible.

Coach's second quandary had to do with his backfield. Ray Coates, Red Knight, Jimmy Cason, and I were all tailbacks. I remember him telling the four of us, "I guess there's no choice with Tittle. He can't run worth a darn and he can't block, so we've *got* to make him the quarterback. At least he can throw the ball pretty well." I was just happy that Bernie thought that much of me!

I remember him telling the four of us, "I guess there's no choice with Tittle. He can't run worth a darn and he can't block, so we've got to make him the quarterback."

Upon revamping the backfield positions, we were ready to put our offense in motion. Red Knight, who was a tremendous runner and quick off the start, became our fullback. Jimmy Cason shared the right halfback position with newcomer Dan Sandifer, and Ray Coates became our left halfback. But even with Carl Brumbaugh at the

32

helm, the T formation was still a strange and difficult concept to understand.

Even after Brumbaugh demonstrated to me what was expected of the quarterback, I was still confused. I scratched my head and said, "How am I going to get back out of there to pass?"

Brumbaugh said, "Oh, you'll get back all right. Don't worry about it. I've never lost a quarterback yet."

Next he lined us up in the T formation. We all felt awkward lined up that way. I had my hands under center Melvin Didier's crotch, and Cason, Knight, and Coates were in a straight line behind me. I had to look over my shoulder to see them. If that wasn't bad enough, I had the defensive middle guard glaring at me from the line. I thought he would run me over for sure.

Right from the beginning I had trouble getting set to throw. Dropping back from center put me off balance, and it was difficult to plant my foot and throw the ball as I had done in the single-wing formation. It was bad enough that I was fumbling all over myself on the drop back, but when I finally was able to get back without stumbling, I couldn't find my receivers or blockers. The single-wing formation allowed me to see everything that was going on right in front of me. The T had me going one way and everyone else the other.

Brumbaugh tried to convince me that I would eventually get the hang of it, but I knew it would take time…and patience.

I eventually learned the T, and it convinced me that dropping back from center is the single most important thing for a quarterback to master. Obviously every quarterback must have a good arm, but even then a quarterback is only as good as his drop back. The T formation requires a quick drop back with no more than a one- or two-second release, and timing is everything.

The T offense in 1945 was quite different than the one that is used today. In 1945 we utilized two tight ends, and everyone was shoulder-to-shoulder. The only split position in motion was the halfback. The first few plays were drives up the middle. Shoulder fakes and hiding the ball were the norm.

As I had mentioned before, Georgia was the only Southeastern Conference team that converted to the T formation. Alabama, Tennessee, Mississippi State, Tulane, and Ole Miss were still running from the single wing.

I remember our first game that year. It was against Rice, and we killed them. I sent Cason in motion to the left, and nobody even went out to cover him. The defense had no idea what was going on. The next play I sent Coates in motion to the right and, like Cason, he was uncovered. All I had to do was lob the ball to either one of them and off they went for the score. The defense never adjusted, and we went on to beat Rice 42–0. I had yet to become a polished T quarterback, but I was getting there.

That year we surprised a lot of teams. Not only did we beat Rice, but we also beat Texas A&M, Georgia, Vanderbilt, Ole Miss, Georgia Tech, and Tulane. Our only losses were to Mississippi State and Alabama—the latter gaining a berth in the Rose Bowl, where they defeated USC 34–14. Georgia, the only other T-formation school, was not surprised by our play calls, but we not only beat them, we shut them out 32–0.

Our overall record for the 1945 season was 7–2, and our conference record was 5–2. We ranked 15th overall in the polls.

The rules of the collegiate game were a lot different back then. For example it was illegal to send information from the sideline to the quarterback. You couldn't hand-signal or send in a substitute to tell you what to do because you could only substitute one time per quarter. If you went out of the ballgame in the first quarter you couldn't come back in until the second quarter. So there was no way to get communication to the quarterback. If you even tried to communicate from the sideline it was a 15-yard penalty for illegal coaching.

The quarterback was also the signal-caller with no help from the sideline. Whenever a substitute came into the huddle the referee would stick his head inside of the huddle with the substitute to be sure that he didn't talk to the quarterback. The substitute couldn't talk to the quarterback until after the first play. That was the rule, and you couldn't call timeout. Let's say it was fourth down and two and you wanted to go for it. If you looked over at the sideline and one of the coaches moved his foot forward, as if to tell you to kick it, your team would be hit with a penalty, and it would cost you 15 yards.

Coach Moore found an ingenious way of communicating with the quarterback without getting caught by the officials. Whenever our team would call a timeout, the water boy would bring 10 or 12 half-pints of water to the huddle. One of the half-pints would have a different-colored cap on it. I knew that one was for the quarterback. When I would pull the cap off it would say something like "Punt on two" or maybe "29 Sweep X Cross" (a pass pattern). The information came from Coach Moore who, of course, was on the sideline.

Coach Moore found an ingenious way of communicating with the quarterback without getting caught by the officials.

I remember playing in one game when it was fourth down with a yard to go. We only had 30 seconds left in the ballgame. Obviously, we needed to make a first down.

I called time and our water boy came out with the water bottles. I opened mine (the one with the green cap), and it said

"Punt." I thought, *This can't be right. Why would we punt the ball with only 30 seconds left in the ballgame when we are behind by six? This is stupid!*

But being the disciplined player that I was, I got in the huddle and said, "Quick kick." Right then all 10 players went crazy. They said, "Are you dumb? What are you talking about—quick kickin' the ball? The score is behind by six!"

"I don't care," I said. "That's what we are supposed to do. We are kicking it!"

We kicked the ball, and it went out of bounds on the 2-yard line. The opposing team got the ball and tried to run an off-tackle play, hoping to kill the clock. They ended up fumbling. We recovered the ball and called timeout. There were nine seconds to go in the game. I threw the winning touchdown pass, and we won the game.

After the game was over, I found out why the coach called for a quick kick. What had happened was that Coach had forgotten to take off the cap and change the play. The play that I had read was from the third quarter when he sent in the play that said "Punt." I thought it was the wrong thing to do but, following orders, I punted.

The next day the newspapers had written that it was the most brilliant call that any quarterback had ever made in the history of LSU. I was a hero. If only they had known…

That year I played quarterback on offense and halfback on defense and averaged 54 minutes per game. I also got to know my center, Melvin Didier, better with each game, but it wasn't until our annual awards dinner in January that I got to meet him face-to-face.

6

1946: A Winning Season

LOUISIANA STATE ENTERED A NEW ERA OF COLLEGIATE FOOTBALL. With the success of the T formation and the end of World War II, competition among college football teams had become intense. The war veterans who were now returning to the college ranks were older, bigger, and faster.

Although change was definitely among us, LSU and its 4-F backfield had a tremendous football team in 1946. Our only loss that season was to Georgia Tech, 26–7. Other than that, Rice was our only close game—we won 7–6. We convincingly beat Mississippi State, Texas A&M, Vanderbilt, Ole Miss, Alabama, Miami (Florida), Fordham, and Tulane by an average of 24 points per game.

Our overall record that year was 9–1–1 and our conference record was 5–1. We were ranked No. 8 in the college polls.

After being ignored by the Sugar Bowl, we were invited to play in the Cotton Bowl against Arkansas on January 1, 1947, in front of 18,000 shivering fans. It was one of the worst, if not the worst, football weather that I had ever played in.

Dallas had been bombarded with heavy rain, sleet, and snow. The gridiron had turned into a sheet of ice, and the footing was extremely treacherous. The only satisfaction I got was knowing that Arkansas was no better off than we were.

We held a 15–1 edge over the Razorbacks in first downs and a 271–54 advantage in total yardage. When the final gun sounded, ending the game, the scoreboard read "LSU 0, Arkansas 0." This scoreless standoff became known as the Ice Bowl.

As I sat in the locker room at the end of the game trying to thaw out, a man walked up to me and said, "Y.A., I'm Creighton Miller of the Cleveland Browns. I'd like to talk to you."

"Sure," I said. "What about?"

"The Cleveland Browns have drafted you, and we'd like you to sign with us," he said.

I was caught off guard with what Mr. Miller told me. I was still a junior. I didn't understand what was going on. I knew nothing of how the professional draft worked, and it seemed to me that drafting a junior would be illegal.

"How can you sign me when I still have another year left?" I asked Mr. Miller.

Miller seemed puzzled by my question.

> *I knew nothing of how the professional draft worked, and it seemed to me that drafting a junior would be illegal.*

"Well, maybe I'd better check into it," he said. "Anyway, you'll be hearing from us."

He shook my hand and exited the locker room. That was the last I saw of him—or heard from the Cleveland Browns organization until a year later when I became eligible for the pro draft.

Many of the other guys on my team would also end up in the professional ranks. Halfback Ray Coates and tackle Ray Collins played with the New York Giants, Jim Cason went to the San Francisco 49ers, and Dan Sandifer played for the Washington Redskins. Ed Champagne was drafted by the Los Angeles Rams, Jeff Burkett played for the Chicago Cardinals, and Hubert Shurtz was a tackle for the Pittsburgh Steelers.

7

1947: The Belt-Buckle Game

WITH OUR PAST RECORD, ONE WOULD HAVE THOUGHT THAT LSU would have had its greatest gridiron year in 1947…but we didn't. Most of our games were close, some too close. We beat Rice, Texas A&M, Boston College, Vanderbilt, and Mississippi State and were defeated by Georgia, Ole Miss, and Alabama. We ended up in a tie against Tulane.

It was a far cry from our 9–1–1 1946 season, and I never understood why we did so poorly. We had a tremendous backfield with Cason, Coates, Sandifer, and Knight and a top offensive line with tackles Ray Collins, Ed Champagne, and Jeff Burkett. But we ended the season 5–3–1 and a bowl invitation was not bestowed upon the 1947 LSU team. Not only was the team disappointed with our poor showing, but so was Coach Moore.

Even though we didn't have a great season, two games from that season will forever stand out in my mind. Unfortunately we didn't win either of them. The first game was played on November 1 at home. It was against Ole Miss, and the winner of that game would get a bowl bid. We ended up losing 20–18. I call this game the Belt-Buckle Game. Not only did we lose, but it turned out to be the most embarrassing incident of my entire football career.

I lost my pants in front of 40,000 fans—one of whom was my fiancée, Minnette DeLoach.

While playing defense, I intercepted a pass from Ole Miss' second-string quarterback. I was playing the left corner and timed the ball perfectly. I cut in front of the Mississippi receiver just as he was reaching for the ball. I grabbed the ball away from him but not before he tackled me around the middle and tore loose my belt buckle.

Back then football pants were not made of Lycra (hell, it wasn't even invented yet) and did not fit tight against the skin. They were somewhat baggy and loose and needed a belt to hold them up.

I had taken only a few steps en route to scoring the winning touchdown when I realized that I was about to lose my pants. I couldn't stop to pull them up. The team needed the six points more than I needed to pull up my pants—even if 40,000 people, including Minnette, were watching.

I tucked the ball under my right arm and held on to my pants with my left hand. There was no one between the goal line and me. I remember first crossing the 50-yard line, then the 40. I was on my way. I wasn't running that fast because, first of all, I'm not that fast to begin with, and second because it was hard to run while holding up my pants.

> *I had taken only a few steps en route to scoring the winning touchdown when I realized that I was about to lose my pants.*

By the time I reached the 20, I had slowed down considerably. A couple of Mississippi defensive backs had a good angle on me, and I was hemmed in along the sideline.

As the nearest back made a grab for me, I tried to shift the ball from my right hand to my left so I could stiff-arm him. In the process, I completely forgot that my left hand was all that stood between me and total embarrassment.

40

As my pants began to slip off my hips, I managed to jog a few more steps as they slid down around my knees. I fell flat on my face, 10 yards away from the winning touchdown. The opposition never laid a finger on me. They didn't have to; I was taken out by my own pants!

I staggered to my feet, frantically trying to pull up my pants, but I fell again. By this time the entire fan base at Tiger Stadium was in an uproar. Everyone was laughing—even my own teammates.

Coates, Cason, and Knight stumbled onto the field to shield me so I could pull up my pants. They continued to laugh uncontrollably.

Losing my pants was not funny to me. I was embarrassed and humiliated. And more than anything else, I was angry because I had failed to get the touchdown. Furthermore, we lost the game.

The second game was my final appearance against Tulane, which ended in a 6–6 tie. I always seemed to play my best against my brother Jack's alma mater.

In 1944 we beat Tulane 25–6. I rotated with the other quarterbacks, but at least I got a chance to play. As a sophomore, I completed 11 of 12 passes for two touchdowns, and the following year I completed eight of nine passes for two more scores. In 1947, my senior year, I completed 10 of 16 passes. In my four years I helped LSU to a 3–0–1 record against Tulane. Every so often I would take the time to remind Jack of that record.

Sometimes a guy can want a win so badly that it can almost ruin his career. Even though this book is about football, I feel it necessary to include this one incident that almost changed my gridiron career—permanently.

During our freshman year, Jim Cason and I tried out for the LSU varsity baseball team. Of course I was a pitcher and I wanted to be the best. On the very first day of batting practice the coach wanted me to ease up on the batters and let them "get a piece of the ball." Being the competitor that I was, there was no way that I was going to let anyone hit the ball. So, without bothering to warm up, I threw the ball as hard as I could to each and every batter. There was no method to my madness—no change-ups, no curves, no control—I just wanted to fire it past them. It was my belief that any pitcher who wanted to get hit wasn't worth a damn anyway.

I was having a great time, when all of a sudden I felt a sharp pain in my right shoulder. I tried to throw the ball again, but it bounced halfway to home plate. Immediately I knew that there was something very wrong. My career was over before it had a chance to begin.

When spring practice came around, my shoulder was still in a lot of pain, but I never told Bernie Moore about it. I really wanted to play but was afraid that Coach would bench me if he felt that I couldn't throw the ball. I toughed out the season, but then disaster struck.

One morning I woke up with such pain in my right shoulder that I could not raise my arm. The pain had extended to my wrist. I can't even begin to tell you how afraid I was. I decided to see a doctor in Baton Rouge instead of our LSU doctor. I knew word would get back to Coach Moore, and I didn't want him to know what was going on.

The doctor told me that I had a growth on my clavicle. It had protruded out so far that it required surgery. He told me that an operation would definitely impair my throwing ability and that the shoulder would be stiff for quite a while. Time was the one thing that I didn't have, so I thanked him and left. At that point, surgery was not an option.

I went and visited another doctor. He told me that deep X-ray treatments might possibly help. Anything was better than surgery, so I gave it a shot. It didn't cure my shoulder, but at least I was able to play football—and at that time, that's all that mattered.

8

1948: The Year of the Quarterback

ON DECEMBER 6, 1947, I THREW MY LAST PASS FOR THE LSU TIGERS. As I previously mentioned, we had just tied Tulane at New Orleans. I was walking off the field when I noticed a familiar face walking toward me. It was Creighton Miller of the Cleveland Browns. He was there to sign me to a professional contract with the club.

Miller didn't waste any time. As soon as the final gun went off, he walked right on to the field to meet me. He and some of the other Cleveland scouts wanted to meet with me at the Roosevelt Hotel in downtown New Orleans to discuss my contract. I told them I would be there.

Back in the locker room, I asked Bernie Moore for advice on the matter. At that time there were two professional leagues, the All-America Football Conference (AAFC) and the National Football League (NFL). I had no knowledge of the player draft, nor did I know why I was the property of the Cleveland Browns and not some other club.

I asked Bernie if I should meet with the Cleveland people, and he advised me to do so. "Go and hear what they have to say, Y.A., but don't sign anything until you have spoken to me first."

I felt more at ease that I had Bernie to help me.

When I arrived at the Roosevelt Hotel, there was no beating around the bush. Miller got right down to the point. "Y.A., we think you are a great passer and that you can be a star in pro football. We are prepared to offer you a contract for $8,000."

Eight thousand dollars was considered a fortune back then. Remembering what Bernie had told me, I said that I would like time to think it over. Miller agreed.

When I saw Bernie the following morning he told me not to sign. "They'll go higher. You are worth more than $8,000," he said.

Miller called me that afternoon. I told him that I had not yet reached a decision. He said that was understandable and then asked me to be a guest of the Browns at the AAFC Championship Game against the Yankees in New York in December.

I had never seen a professional game, and I quickly agreed to his offer.

I flew to New York and was introduced to the Cleveland coach, Paul Brown. He was cordial but not friendly. I guess that was because he had an important upcoming game to think about, so I could hardly expect him to spend a lot of time with me.

At that time the team was working out for its big game against the Yankees. Their practice was held at Macombs Dam Park. That was the first time I saw the big tackle from Notre Dame, George Connor. George would eventually end up with the Chicago Bears.

Both of us stood there in awe as we watched the great Cleveland quarterback, Otto Graham, and the best fullback in all of football, Marion Motley, show what they did best.

The next day I sat with Connor on the Cleveland bench at Yankee Stadium as the Browns defeated the New York Yanks 14–3 to win the league championship.

The game really wasn't that exciting, but the thrill of watching the pros made me realize that they were much bigger, faster, and smarter at the game of football than the guys in the collegiate ranks. Otto Graham and Marion Motley were just as good if not better than their legends. Paul Brown was an exceptional coach, and Cleveland proved that by the way they played and the few mistakes that they made.

The New York lineup was comprised of the great halfback Buddy Young plus Tom Landry, Otto Schnellbacher, Arnie Weinmeister, Bruce Alford, Jack Russell, and Martin Ruby. The following year I ended up playing against all of them, with the exception of Weinmeister.

After the game I met with Coach Brown. Instead of the original $8,000 that had been offered to me, Brown raised the proposal to $10,000 with a $2,000 bonus if I signed with Cleveland. I had no alternative but to sign. That was big money!

With money in my pocket and a contract with the Browns, I returned to LSU to complete the spring semester. I quickly found out that I was not the only "pro" on campus. Jim Cason had signed with the San Francisco 49ers, Piggy Barnes was the property of the Philadelphia Eagles, Hubert Shurtz was now a Pittsburgh Steeler, and Dan Sandifer contracted with the Washington Redskins.

I finally graduated in early June 1948. A week later, on June 20, I married my high school sweetheart, Minnette. I was raised as a Methodist and Minnette was a Presbyterian, but as an old Southern custom we were married in her family's Presbyterian church in Marshall. We honeymooned near the Gulf Coast, through Mississippi, and completed our trip with a short stay at a Louisiana plantation owned by an aunt of Minnette's.

Throughout this time period, professional football was being reshaped and recreated through a series of events that would have a major impact on my football career.

Here I am in 1941 as a freshman at Marshall High School. I continued to be their quarterback for all four years. In 1942 I was named the Marshall Mavericks' Most Valuable Player.

From 1944 through 1947 I played football for Louisiana State University. I played tailback in my first year and then switched to the then-new T formation, where I made All Southeastern Conference in 1946 and 1947.

I was first drafted by Cleveland in the 1948 draft, but my contract was given to the Baltimore Colts in order to strengthen the league of the AAFC. I played for the Colts for three years before coming to San Francisco and playing with the 49ers. Both of these shots are 49ers PR photos of me in 1952.

1952 vs. the Lions in Detroit. Here I am scoring for the 49ers with Detroit's Jack Christiansen holding on tight. It was on this play that I suffered a triple cheekbone fracture when Jim David's knee slammed into my face as he tackled me. We ended up beating the Lions 24–0.

San Francisco 49ers captain Bob St. Clair hands me the game ball after a 1957 victory.

The Million Dollar Backfield circa 1957–1958. This is the only complete backfield in the Pro Football Hall of Fame. From left to right: myself, Joe Perry, Hugh McElhenny, and John Henry Johnson.

1950s 49ers group photo. From left to right: Charlie Powell, unknown player, myself, Joe Arenas, John Henry Johnson, Hugh McElhenny (in back), Matt Hazeltine, unknown player, Joe Perry, and Bill Jessup.

I was traded from the 49ers to the New York Giants in 1961. I played four years with New York. In this 1962 photo we were playing the Redskins at DC Stadium. We beat them 42–24.

Giants head coach Allie Sherman gives me some advice on the sideline during our December 31, 1961, game against the Packers at Milwaukee County Stadium.

In 1964 this photo was selected as the Photo of the Century by Sports Illustrated.
Moments before the shot was snapped by Morris Berman of the Pittsburgh Post-
Gazette, *I had been pounded to the turf by 270-pound defensive end John Baker
of the Pittsburgh Steelers. My fluttering pass had landed in the arms of a surprised
Steelers tackle, Chuck Hinton, who returned the interception eight yards into the
end zone for a touchdown. It was a heck of a way to get famous!*

I was the offensive consultant with the San Francisco 49ers from 1965 to 1969.

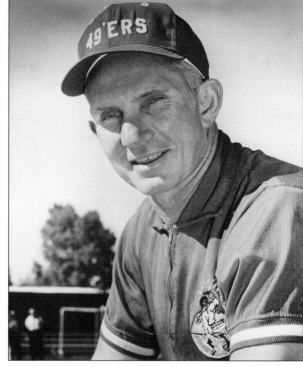

Being inducted into the Pro Football Hall of Fame in 1971 in Canton, Ohio, was my greatest thrill. All my children were there to witness me going into the Hall. It is a moment that I will never forget.

The Million Dollar Backfield at the Pro Football Hall of Fame, where we celebrated 50 years together. From left to right: Joe Perry, John Henry Johnson, Hugh McElhenny, and me.

Here I am on the set of the movie Any Given Sunday *with Terry Bradshaw (far left) and Dick Butkus (center). Butkus, Bob St. Clair, Johnny Unitas, and I all played opposing head coaches opposite Al Pacino.*

Second Quarter

The Colts, the 49ers, and the Giants

9

In the Blink of an Eye— from Cleveland to Baltimore

ALL-AMERICA FOOTBALL CONFERENCE COMMISSIONER Admiral Jonas Ingram announced that the Baltimore Colts franchise was in financial distress and if they didn't raise enough money to retain the franchise, the league would take it over. Baltimore's business leaders formed a Save the Colts Committee and raised over $200,000 to bankroll the team for at least another year.

Even though the Baltimore administration had been revamped and replaced by men who "could do the job," the Colts still needed more in the area of player personnel. Admiral Ingram hired Ben Lindheimer—owner of the Los Angeles Rams—and Paul Brown as directors. Their job was to study and evaluate the Colts' player-personnel problems and suggest how to strengthen the Baltimore team with players from other AAFC teams.

A list of prominent AAFC starters was made available to Baltimore. New York Yank all-league tackle Dick Barwegen and end Ollie Poole were the first to go. The Rams sent tackles Pete Berezney and Lee Artoe. Cleveland gave up one of the AAFC's best tackles, Ernie Blandin, and halfback Mickey Mayne along with a rookie by the name of Y.A. Tittle.

Before I could even get one play in, I was traded from the best team in the league to the worst—the Baltimore Colts.

After its first year, the league faced a few difficult changes. Jim Crowley gave up his commissionership to take the head coaching job with the Chicago Rockets, a team plagued by financial and management instability. Admiral Jonas H. Ingram took his place as head of the league. The Buffalo Bisons were renamed the Buffalo Bills. And the bankrupt Miami Seahawks organization was purchased and moved to Baltimore by a group led by Bob Rodenberg. The new team, named the Colts, played its home games at Municipal Stadium, which, appropriately enough, was shaped like a horseshoe.

> *Before I could even get one play in, I was traded from the best team in the league to the worst—the Baltimore Colts.*

The team, led by former Green Bay Packers player and Purdue head coach Cecil Isbell and quarterbacked by Bud Schwenk, a former NFL player, went a miserable 2–11–1. What Baltimore needed most was a quarterback. Coach Isbell was determined not to repeat in 1948.

Isbell's first choice for quarterback was my former roommate at Mrs. Poole's boarding house, Bobby Layne. Coach flew down to Austin and met with Bobby. He spread 10 new $1,000 bills on a bed and told Bobby that it could all be his just for saying yes. Layne later told me that his eyes had nearly popped out of his head.

Isbell also offered him a three-year contract—$20,000 the first year, $22,000 the second year, and $25,000 the third year. Bobby told Isbell he would sign the following day, but before the dawn of the following morning, Layne had decided not to take the Colts up on their offer. It seems that he spoke with his former Texas coach, D.X. Bible, and he advised Bobby that he might do better with the Chicago Bears, an *established* team in the NFL, than with the Colts, who were part of an unsettled league.

Even though Chicago had the great Sid Luckman and Johnny Lujack from Notre Dame, George Halas still wanted Layne. Isbell tried four more times to persuade Bobby to sign with Baltimore, but he refused.

Fate seems to play an important role in our lives. What would have become of me if Bobby had signed with the Colts? We would have been competing against each other as we did four years prior at the University of Texas. And what would have happened to me if I had stayed with Cleveland? I would have had to compete against Otto Graham—when he was in his prime! I would have ended up on the bench, a place that I never wanted to be.

So I wasn't really disappointed when I received the letter from the Browns saying that I had been traded to Baltimore. I just wanted the opportunity to play pro football. Coach Isbell sweetened the deal by calling me and assuring me that I had a good chance of becoming the Colts' No. 1 quarterback. Bud Schwenk had been cut. My only competition would come from Charlie O'Rourke, who was traded by the Los Angeles Dons to help the Colts rebuild their team.

I was thankful that the Cleveland letter came when it did. Half of my bonus money had been spent on a new car, and the other half was spent on our honeymoon. I was virtually broke and needed to report to Baltimore immediately.

I kissed Minnette good-bye—as I did every July since—and flew to Chicago. In Chicago I boarded a train to Sun Valley, Idaho, where the Colts held their training camp.

When I arrived in Sun Valley I thought I was in paradise, as did the rest of the team.

When I arrived in Sun Valley I thought I was in paradise, as did the rest of the team. We lived in Swiss chalets, ate great food, and attended parties where beautiful young waitresses served us food and drink.

My roommate was Windell Williams from Rice University. He was in awe of the campsite. I remember his first words to me were, "How long has this been going on?"

The entire team felt the same way. The Colts were Sun Valley's biggest attraction that summer. Our daily practice sessions overflowed with tourists trying to get a glimpse of the players. This made us all feel really important. At times it was difficult to remember that we were there to play football.

Little did I know that I would be in for one big surprise. When I arrived at training camp, there were a total of four quarterbacks! Besides O'Rourke and me, there was Dick Working from Virginia and Rex Olson from Brigham Young. Olson had been rated the No. 3 passer in the nation the year before.

I questioned John Sanborne as to what Coach Isbell was going to do with all the quarterbacks. His response was short and to the point: "He's going to cut most of them."

I didn't expect that as an answer. It really took me aback. After being the No. 1 quarterback at LSU for the past four years, I somehow thought that it would be the same in the pros. Coach Isbell (after our initial talk) had given me the impression that O'Rourke and I would be the only two Baltimore quarterbacks. That proved not to be the case when I had to wait in line for my turn to throw a few passes in practice.

1948 proved to be the Year of the Quarterback for professional football. The University of Texas sent Bobby Layne to the Bears as did Notre Dame with their All-American, Johnny Lujack; Mississippi's Charlie Conerly signed with the Giants; and Alabama's Harry Gilmer joined Sammy Baugh and the Washington Redskins.

Each of these men played in the 1947 Chicago College All-Star Game. I was selected to play, but a pulled leg muscle kept me from going. Back then, any college All-Star player who had signed with a professional team reported to camp first, then played in the game. Today the player plays in the All-Star Game first and then reports to camp afterward.

Halfway though the preseason it was evident that the two quarterbacks would be O'Rourke and me. Even though I had played a great deal during this time, it was obvious that Coach Isbell had chosen Charlie as his No. 1 passer. Even though O'Rourke and I remained good friends, the rivalry between us was evident.

I guess it was my nature to become friends with my rival quarterback teammates, and I continued to do so throughout my career. In San Francisco it was that way with Frankie Albert and Earl Morral, and it was the same in New York with Charlie Conerly.

But when it came to which quarterback would sit on the bench, friendship took a backseat. I never wanted my rival to be throwing touchdowns while I sat on the bench. Of course I wanted my team to win, but in the back of my mind I secretly hoped that our scores would come by a run or by an interception from our defense—never from a pass by my rival.

Even though the majority of the team comprised rookies, our 1948 Baltimore team proved to be a good one. Ends Windell Williams, Johnny North from Vanderbilt, and Hub Bechtol from Texas were great when it came to catching the ball; Ernie Blandin from the Browns and Dick Barwegan from the Giants strengthened and secured our offensive line; and Al Klug from Marquette and Barry French from Perdue were terrific guards. Lamar "Racehorse" Davis, Bus Mertes, Mickey Mayne, Billy Hillenbrand, and Aubrey Fowler made up the backfield.

Our first preseason game was in Portland, Oregon, against the Los Angeles Dons. With only a few minutes remaining in the fourth quarter, the Dons were winning 19–7. I was sitting on the bench next to my roommate, Windell Williams, when I jokingly said, "If they don't get me in there soon, we're going to lose this thing. Isbell is going to blow this thing unless he puts me in there."

Just then, Coach waved me off the bench and said, "Get in there for O'Rourke." I doubt that Isbell overheard my remarks; I just think he wanted me to get a few plays in before the final whistle.

I jumped off the bench and ran on to the field. It was as though the stars and planets had aligned themselves perfectly. We took the ball and—boom!—we went in for a score. We stopped the Dons after the kickoff and continued to march down the field. I continued to call timeouts and threw sideline passes to stop the clock. We worked our way all the way to the Los Angeles 20, but it was too little too late. When the final gun sounded, ending the game, it was Los Angeles who came out the victor. Final score: Dons 19, Colts 14.

After the game, Windell went and told everyone, "Y.A. said that we would lose if Isbell didn't put him in the game. He almost pulled it out. If only Coach had put him in sooner."

A few sportswriters overheard Windell running off at the mouth and decided to play up the story in the next day's paper. Coach never said a word to me, but from then on, I watched what I said—especially around Windell.

The following week we were trounced by the San Francisco 49ers. It was then that I first experienced the wrath of coach Cecil Isbell. He was so upset by our performance that day that he left Kezar Stadium and immediately put the team on a plane. We flew all night long and landed in Toledo, Ohio, in the wee hours of the morning. The team walked off the plane and on to a bus for a grueling ride to Adrien College in Adrien, Michigan, where Isbell had set up training camp.

Coach was so upset about our loss to San Francisco that he directed the bus driver to drive us *directly* to the practice field— forfeiting our stop at the college to drop off our gear.

When we pulled up to the field, Isbell shouted for us to disembark the bus. He had us line up and yelled, "Now you are going to run and run and run." With that he blew his whistle and we began running wind sprints. We sprinted 10 then jogged 10. We were lucky that nobody dropped dead from the torrid heat and humidity! At the end, we were absolutely exhausted, not to mention mad as hell.

The team thought they had already served out their punishment by performing in the previous night's marathon, but upon returning to practice the following day, we found out that it was just the beginning of Coach's sadistic punishment.

He had ordered that we suit up in full gear for the morning workout. Full gear? Nobody ever does that less than two days after a game. This was insane!

Coach had us scrimmage that day for a total of six full quarters. We were literally ready to drop. Guys began to develop bruises on top of the bruises from the injuries we had sustained in the game against San Francisco. There wasn't one guy on the team who didn't hurt from his head to his toes.

We were all so exhausted that we could have cared less if we ever saw another football field again.

Isbell finally blew the whistle to end practice, and each of us, one by one, crawled back to the dorm. We were all so exhausted that we could have cared less if we ever saw another football field again.

The following Wednesday we were scheduled to play the AAFC champion Cleveland Browns in Toledo. By some miracle, we ended up beating them 21–17. That morning we could barely get out of bed, much less play football, but we did, and we prevailed over the best team in football in our final exhibition game of the 1948 season.

The 1948 Baltimore Colts did not resemble the 1947 Baltimore Colts at all. And considering the team's record from the year before, that was probably a good thing—and maybe, just maybe, Coach Isbell really did know what he was doing!

10

Baltimore: A Real Football Town

WHEN THE TEAM ARRIVED HOME TO BALTIMORE after beating the Cleveland Browns in Toledo, there were thousands of fans lined up at the airport to greet us. They were shouting, cheering, and carrying signs. There was even a big parade down Main Street for the team. All this for winning a preseason game. I pondered as to what Baltimore would be like if we won a championship. It would go absolutely wild!

I quickly found out that Colts fans were this loyal whether we won or lost. They loved their Baltimore team. If you played football for the Colts you were definitely considered a celebrity. I liked that.

In the past I had always thought of Baltimore as a baseball town. They just about owned the city back in the day. Long before the Colts had even come into existence, the Boys of Summer had heroes like Wee Willie Keeler, Hughie Jennings, and the fiery John McGraw. Their names were known throughout the country. But in 1948 all of that would change. The Colts were now the darlings of Baltimore, and the fans made even a rookie like me feel important.

The best description I ever heard about Baltimore being a football town was said by Tarzan White, an assistant coach with the Colts in 1947. Watching the fans go wild over their team at a home game, he exclaimed, "This place is like a big Green Bay!"

Anyone who is familiar with the loyalty and devotion of the die-hard fans of Green Bay fully understand White's quote.

I myself have a personal, vested interest with the fans of Baltimore. When the Colts franchise disbanded in 1951 I was drafted by the San Francisco 49ers. When we played the Eagles in Philadelphia, over a thousand Baltimore fans came to see me play against Philly. They sat right behind the 49ers bench and cheered me on. It gave me a warm feeling to know that I had not been forgotten by them.

Soon after my arrival in Baltimore, Minnette and her dad drove to Maryland to meet me. Our mission was to find an apartment, which at that time was not an easy task to complete. World War II had just ended and nothing was available.

One day Windell Williams, Ollie Poole, and I were told of an apartment that was available on the other side of town. The problem was that there was only *one* apartment and there were three of us. I told Minnette to wait while the three of us drove down to look at the place.

The apartment was nice but small. We decided to flip a coin to see who would get it. I won. I couldn't wait to tell Minnette the good news.

We decided to flip a coin to see who would get it. I won.

We moved all our belongings in the same day. After unpacking, Minnette decided to take a shower. After walking around the apartment for a minute or so, she stopped and asked me, "Where is it?"

"Where is what?" I replied.

"The shower!" she said as her voice began to take on a high pitch.

I stopped to think for a moment. I didn't remember seeing any bathroom in the apartment, and in our haste to move in I just didn't think about it.

"Have you tried the bathroom?" I said, not trying to sound sarcastic.

"Yes, I did, and it's not there—not even a bathtub!"

I immediately called the landlady, who lived upstairs. She told me that the shower was located in the basement behind the hot-water boiler.

Annoyed, I said, "Well, that's a fine place for a shower! Why didn't you tell us it was in the basement?"

"You didn't ask," she said.

That ended that conversation!

Minnette and I got used to taking showers in the cellar. The only time it became difficult was during the winter months. It was extremely cold.

The 1948 season in Baltimore will always remain special to me. We lived in a great sports town with fans who loved us. Most of the guys on the roster had been married less than six months. We all hung around together as a team and with our families. It was a wonderful time. The Colts were winning and had yet to experience defeat.

A few days before we played our opener on September 5 against the New York Yanks, who had been the Eastern Conference champions a year before, Isbell told the newspapers that I would be starting at the quarterback position.

The response from the media was not well taken. Charlie O'Rourke had started most of the preseason games, and between he and I he was the more experienced player.

But Isbell stayed true to his word and was willing to take a chance on a green, inexperienced quarterback. My hope was that I could justify his faith in me.

That season-opener game at Memorial Stadium is one that I will never forget. We crushed the Yankees 45–28 and I broke four All-America conference records that day. It was one of those days where everything seemed to go right. I completed 11 of 20 passes for 346 yards and averaged 3.5 yards on my completions and 16.5 yards for every pass attempt. I threw for five touchdowns and handed off once to Billy Hillenbrand for the sixth. Even though I received a lot of ink that day, it was definitely a combined effort for the win. Our defense savagely tackled the Yanks' great halfback, Buddy Young, and put him out of commission. Spec Sanders was stopped dead every time he got the ball. The offensive line protected me from Arnie Weinmeister and the other New York pass rushers. Not only was it a combined effort, but it was a tribute to Isbell and his fine coaching staff.

A few weeks later we went to New York to once again play the Yankees, and again we beat them, 27–14, proving that our last win wasn't just a fluke. During that same road trip we also routed Brooklyn. Going into October, this Baltimore Colts team was leading the Eastern Division by one full game. Not bad for a team that only won three games in 1947 and, on top of it all, almost lost their franchise.

Our next game was against the Cleveland Browns, and we knew that it was going to be a tough one. When we arrived at the field on that cold and stormy Tuesday night, it had already been raining two days straight. There was talk of cancelling the game, but unlike baseball not rain, sleet, or snow could postpone this gridiron matchup. The Browns wanted payback for the previous year in Toledo when we beat them. We welcomed the challenge. If we beat Cleveland, we would bust open the Eastern Division race.

The conditions of the field were horrific. Everything was flooded and the winds were blowing so hard that you couldn't see three feet in front of your face.

Before the kickoff Isbell warned me that points were going to be difficult to make. That was obvious. I didn't need him to tell me that. I also knew that the team who scored first would be more or less in command of the game—and that score needed to happen early in the game because conditions would worsen as the game progressed.

Everything was flooded and the winds were blowing so hard that you couldn't see three feet in front of your face.

On the third play of the game we marched down the field to the Baltimore 22. I called a screen pass to Hillenbrand, who caught the ball, picked up his two screen blockers, and went all the way for a touchdown. Rex Grossman kicked the PAT, and we were up by seven with only two minutes gone in the first quarter.

Later that same period, Cleveland fought back in the muddy terrain and came up with a score by Edgar "Special Delivery" Jones to tie the game. But no sooner did they score than Grossman kicked a 40-yard field goal against the wind to put us once more in the lead. The score remained 10–7 as both teams slugged it out in the mud. It wasn't until late in the fourth quarter that the game turned around.

We were on our own 10 when O'Rourke got off a bad punt, which put the Browns on our 27-yard line. With only two minutes left in the game, Otto Graham passed once to Mac Speedie for 21 yards and then pounded the last nail in the coffin with a touchdown pass to Dub Jones for the win. Final score: Cleveland 14, Colts 10.

Cleveland coach Paul Brown referred to the win as "one of the hardest games ever played in his entire career," but that didn't ease our pain from the loss. It did, however, gain us a little more respect in the AAFC.

After the loss to the Browns, the Colts went on to defeat Los Angeles, Chicago, Brooklyn, and Buffalo. Since the Bills were beaten 33–15 in the last game of the season, a playoff game was set up for the Eastern Division title between Baltimore and Buffalo—both having 7–7 records. The winner would face off with the Western Division title winners, the Cleveland Browns. The Baltimore fans began to chant, "Championship, championship!"

Five days before our game with Buffalo, I was summoned to a players' meeting after practice. I sensed something was wrong, and it was.

The veterans of the game felt that the team should get their share of the gate receipts since there was no provision in their contract to cover the possibility of a playoff. Tempers flared, and finally Ernie Blandin and Dick Barwegen were employed to convey the team's demands to Colts president Jake Embry and Colts general manager Walter Driskill.

After listening to Blandin and Barwegen, Embry explained the position of the front office. "We feel a divisional playoff is part of a player's regular contract. Also, we are having a difficult time staying in the black. This extra game could put us on solid ground. We would appreciate the players' understanding in this matter."

Blandin explained that if the players didn't get a portion of the gate receipts there would be a possibility of a strike on Sunday, but his proclamation fell on deaf ears.

Both Blandin and Barwegen reiterated the requests of the front office to the players, who at this point insisted on a strike if their demands weren't met.

Word got back to Embry and Driskill. Embry told the team, "If you don't want to play the game, we will announce to the public that the title has been forfeited to Buffalo. We will consider the season over, and we will all go home."

A second players' meeting was called to vote on whether to play or not. The vote was in, and the decision to play was announced. There was much resentment within the team after that day.

The stage was now set, and the Colts met the Buffalo Bills in Baltimore on December 12.

The Colts drew first blood with a field goal by Grossman, but then Buffalo scored on a pass from Ratterman to O'Connor. The score remained 7–3 throughout the first half.

Baltimore dominated the third quarter. After marching 71 yards downfield, Bus Mertes scored on a nine-yard run. Grossman kicked the conversion and we were up 10–7. Next we marched 87 yards, and again Mertes scored, this time on a one-yard run with Grossman contributing the extra point. The score was 17–7.

In the fourth quarter Ratterman and Bill Gompers connected on a 66-yard scoring pass to cut our lead by three. The Bills regained possession late in the fourth quarter. It was a race against the clock.

After Ratterman had picked up two first downs—one due to an offside penalty—he lobbed the ball to Chet Mutryn, who took three steps and then dropped the ball when he was slammed by Sam Vacanti and Barwegen. One of our tackles, John Mellus, recovered the ball as it bounced down the field, scooped it up, and headed for the Buffalo end zone. He stopped after hearing the frantic whistle of head linesman Tommy Whelan. It was ruled that Mutryn never had possession of the ball, making it an incomplete pass instead of a fumble, therefore returning the ball to Buffalo. Six plays later the Bills scored the winning touchdown on a pass from Ratterman to Baldwin.

With only two and a half minutes left to play in the game, I felt we had enough time to score one more time, but one of my passes that was intended for Davis was intercepted by Buffalo's Ed Hirsch, and he ran it back for six points. Final score: Buffalo 18, Baltimore 17.

When the final gun sounded, the irate Colts fans stormed the field. Their target was head linesman Tommy Whelan. They

When the final gun sounded, the irate Colts fans stormed the field.

were furious about the call he had made earlier in the quarter. Extra police were brought on to the field to protect Whelan from the crowd. Both Buffalo and Colts players escorted the head linesman to the dressing room through the hostile, bottle-throwing crowd. When he finally got inside, I noticed that he had a swollen eye and his mouth had been cut. The mob had even torn the back of his shirt. I know he was scared half to death, and I didn't blame him one bit.

Even though the police tried to calm down the angry mob, they continued yelling for Whelan: "Let's get Whelan! Let's get Whelan!"

It was the wildest, not to mention scariest, professional football game that I had ever encountered. Fistfights arose throughout the stadium as did fires in the stands. People were being knocked down. They protested outside the Stadium Administration Building and refused to move until Whelan came out.

Whelan and the Bills team were huddled inside the building trying to come up with a way to elude the frenzied mob outside. They were finally able to smuggle out the head linesman among the Buffalo players. They all made it safely to their chartered bus right under the noses of those insane fans.

All in all 1948 was a good season for me—a memorable season. I received Rookie of the Year honors in the All-America Conference. Although receiving the honor, I was still deprived of my opportunity to win a championship. The desire to win a world title would eventually become an insidious disease that would continue to plague me in the years to come.

11

Cecil Isbell: The Man Who Taught Me How to Pass

I CREDIT CECIL ISBELL WITH MY SUCCESS AS A FORWARD PASSER. Over the years there had been many coaches who had taken part in my development as a passer, but it was Coach Isbell who molded me into a professional quarterback.

In the beginning it was Joe Magrill at Marshall High who gave me the confidence in my ability to do well. Cracker Brown gave me the okay to "go ahead and throw the ball." Otis Mitchell taught me to be a winner, and Bernie Moore educated me to use my head as well as my arm. But it was Isbell who told me, "There is only one way to play the game of football—throw the damned ball!"

Cecil Isbell had played for the Green Bay Packers under coach Curly Lambeau. Coach Lambeau credits Isbell as a master passer who was a better quarterback than both Sid Luckman and Sammy Baugh. His main receiver was Don Hutson, and in their day there wasn't a combination in the league that could surpass them.

Coach Isbell once told me, "Depend on yourself to complete the pass. Depend on your arm to get the ball to your receiver. Do not rely on pass patterns to miraculously work someone into the clear. Do not expect the defense to make a mistake. Completed passes do not just happen. They are made by the passer and by his receiver, man-to-man. Your job is to get the ball to your receiver, and his job is to catch it. That is what you are paid to do."

My style was to bounce back in the pocket and hit my receiver on a quick square-out instead of waiting for a lot of other things to happen. If my receiver and I couldn't beat them on a square-out, well, then I would beat them down-and-in. It was me and my receiver. I depended on him to whip his man out there in the secondary by a step or maybe by two steps if he was lucky, and then I depended on my right arm to hit him with the pass. I didn't want to be in the position of standing back there waiting for a pattern to open up so I could drop the ball in my receiver's lap.

I've heard people say of other quarterbacks, "He's good at picking out his receivers."

That's crazy! If I have just three seconds to back away from the center, set up, and throw the football, I am not going to back-pedal seven yards and waste time looking around for someone to throw the ball to. I want someone open right away, and if I find him not to be open, I want a No. 2 choice. If my second choice is covered, then I am going to end up throwing the ball away.

In the huddle, I might call my tight end on a square-out 12 yards deep. My No. 2 receiver is going down-and-in, say, 20 yards. Now if my tight end runs his pattern and beats his man, he is going to get that ball. I am going to throw it to him in a hurry. My No. 2 receiver may be down there all by himself, but he is not going to get the ball because my tight end was my No. 1 choice. If my No. 1 receiver could not get free, then I would go to my No. 2 receiver if he was open. The gist of my passing philosophy is this: No. 1, No. 2, or throw the ball away!

I have never been one of those quarterbacks who fades back with the idea of looking at two or three different receivers and finally throwing to the one that is open. You can hit only one man on a pass, and you have to depend on your arm to get the ball out to him—not on some razzle-dazzle pass pattern that suddenly springs a receiver into a hole in the secondary where nobody is covering him.

I have never been one of those quarterbacks who fades back with the idea of looking at two or three different receivers and finally throwing to the one that is open.

This was Cecil Isbell's concept of utilizing the forward pass, and it has been mine ever since I played for him as a rookie with Baltimore in 1948.

Isbell was a great coach and an even greater human being. He remained one of my greatest fans.

At times, after seeing me play a Giants game on television, he would call or write me to say that I was not taking a deep enough pass drop or that perhaps I was moving out of the pass pocket. When we played the Cleveland Browns at Yankee Stadium in 1963, Cecil called me and said, "Y.A., you are sending too many guys out of the backfield. You'd better keep a couple of those big backs in there and let them block for you. Remember, you only need one open receiver to complete the pass."

After studying the films of that Cleveland game, I saw that Isbell had been right—as usual. I had been sending too many backs out as receivers, and the Browns were barreling through the line and pressuring me. The next time we met Cleveland I kept my backs in, and the Browns never once laid a hand on me. We beat them 33–6.

But for all the good that Coach Isbell did for this Baltimore team, 1949 was to become the year of his demise.

Upon returning to the Colts for my second season, the entire front office, staff, coaches, and players were under the false assumption that this would be a great year for the Baltimore organization. We had come so close to winning in '48 that anyone who even dared suggest that the Colts might not win the title would have been tarred and feathered and thrown into Chesapeake Bay.

The new team president, Walter Driskill, stood up at training camp and blatantly stated, "Baltimore will win the All-America Conference championship this year!"

At the beginning of the season it looked like Driskill's prophecy would become a reality. We opened the preseason against the Buffalo Bills and defeated them by a score of 28–12. We were on our way...or so we thought.

Our next four games were played on the road, and we lost every one of them. None of the scores were even close. We were beaten in San Francisco 31–17, annihilated in Los Angeles 45–17, shut out in Cleveland 21–0, and embarrassed by the weak Chicago Hornets 35–7.

The following day, after our loss to Chicago, the Colts' board of directors fired Isbell. President and general manager Walter Driskill became our new coach. Could you imagine that happening in today's NFL?

Our next four games were played on the road, and we lost every one of them.

If I remember correctly, Driskill and Isbell were good friends, and Walter did not want to succeed him. He felt that Cecil received a bad deal from the board for something that was not his fault.

Isbell took his release very badly—so badly that he completely withdrew from people. He was a sensitive and sympathetic man with a great deal of pride. Even though he and Driskill remained friends, he never got over the firing.

As for my personal relationship with Walter, we were not exactly the best of friends. A few weeks before he was named the new coach, he and I were involved in some extremely heated contract discussions. This whole issue with the firing of Coach Isbell was a shock to the team and not an easy adjustment for me to make.

The first team we played against under our new coach was the Cleveland Browns. I never knew why, but Driskill always seemed to be irritated with me—so irritated that he started Sam Vacanti at quarterback. We lost that game 14–13. After that came our only win of the 1949 season—a 35–28 win over the Bills in Buffalo. From that point on we managed to lose every game for the remainder of the season—to the Yanks 24–21, to the Hornets 17–7, to the Yanks again 21–14, to San Francisco 27–10, to the Dons 11–10, and finally to the Bills 18–14.

Throughout the last half of the 1949 season, I felt that the failure of the team was mostly due to my failure on the field. At least that's the way Coach Driskill made it seem. He and I had failed to communicate with one another. It got so bad that I was even afraid to call a play for fear that it would be the "wrong" one.

It seemed as though he was on my back all the time. During film sessions, Driskill never failed to direct his frustrations toward me by shouting, "What play was that, Tittle?" My response was, "Gee, Coach, I'm not sure. Could you run it again?" But he never did, nor did he say anything. The film projector just kept grinding away as we silently watched the Colts being defeated by everyone else in the league. All I could do was slump down in my chair and wait to hear what I would be blamed for next. By this time my self-confidence was all but lost.

But whatever the case and regardless of whose fault it was, the fact remained that the 1949 Colts were really a bad team. I could never really figure it out. We had the same player personnel as we did the year before—Lamar, Davis, Ernie Blandin, Dick

Barwegen, Barry French, Rex Grossman, Johnny North, Bob Nowaskey, Stormy Pfohl, and my roommate, Windell Williams. We also had a lot of new players on the team—rookies, vets, and a few walk-ons. One of these guys was a flashy halfback from St. Mary's by the name of Herman Wedemeyer. Driskill acquired him from the Los Angeles Dons in a somewhat unusual deal.

The Dons had some great backs in George Tagliaferro, Glenn Dobbs, Hosea Rodgers, and others. Wedemeyer, who was a terrific open-field runner and an exciting player to watch, was on the bench. The 49ers wanted Wedemeyer because he had played his college ball in the Bay Area, but the Dons and San Francisco were bitter rivals. Los Angeles refused to send Herman to the north—instead, they cut a deal with Baltimore.

When Driskill had inquired how much Wedemeyer was making, he was in for a surprise. His contract called for $12,000, which was far more than Driskill was willing to pay. Instead the Dons made the Colts an offer that was too good to refuse. They told Driskill that Los Angeles would be willing to pay $3,000 if the Colts would pick up the remaining $9,000. It was agreed. It was probably the only time in NFL history that one team paid another team to take an All-American halfback off its roster. But even with Herman on the team, the Colts finished off the 1949 season with one win and 11 losses.

It was probably the only time in NFL history that one team paid another team to take an All-American halfback off its roster.

It was at this time that the chairman of the board, Charles P. McCormick, announced that the team had lost over $100,000 in revenue that year. This was the same team that Driskill had predicted would win the league championship.

12

The Disbanding of the Colts Franchise

THE PAST YEAR HAD SEEN MANY CHANGES IN PROFESSIONAL football. The All-America Conference had disbanded and Baltimore, along with Cleveland and San Francisco, was now a part of the National Football League. Team president Walter Driskill resigned in May and hired Abraham Warner to take his place. He literally saved the Baltimore franchise.

A new coach by the name of Clem Crowe, who had coached at Buffalo in the 1949 season, was brought in to replace Walter Driskill. Unfortunately his record was no better than Driskill's had been in 1949—where we had lost 11 out of 12 games. In 1950 we lost big—I mean really big! We lost to Los Angeles 70–27, to the Cardinals 55–13, to the Giants 55–20, to the Yanks 51–14, to the Lions 45–21, to the Redskins 38–14, to the Browns 31–0, and to the Eagles 24–14. Our preseason game against the Rams should have been an omen of things to come—they killed us 70–21.

But in all fairness, it was not Clem Crowe's fault. There were many other factors that contributed to the demise of the Colts.

A total of 13 clubs had survived when the All-America Conference and the National Football League decided to merge. With an unbalanced schedule, the NFL designated the 13th club as a swing team that would play each of the other 12 clubs only once instead of twice. Baltimore became the unlucky 13th team.

Another factor had to do with how the NFL distributed talent from the now-defunct New York Yankees and Buffalo Bills. The Colts were once again left out in the cold. The Giants received Arnie Weinmeister, Tom Landry, Otto Schnellbacher, and three other players from the Yanks. Cleveland got the best of the deal, taking John Kissell, Rex Bumgardner, and Abe Gibron from Buffalo. This all came about *before* the other clubs had a chance to pick the surplus AAFC players in an open draft. To this day, I don't understand how they got away with it.

> *Baltimore became the unlucky 13th team.*

Not only did the Colts need help, but so did the Green Bay Packers. We were considered the have-not clubs, while the Browns and Giants just kept getting richer. We did, though, get Chet Mutryn, a fine halfback from the Bills, but it would take a hell of a lot more than one player for the Colts to be considered a contender in 1950.

In my opinion, the group of players who reported to the Baltimore Colts training camp in Westminster, Maryland, in the summer of 1950 might have constituted the worst professional football team in history, and regrettably I was one of them!

Morale was exceptionally low at training camp that year. Coach Crowe had been told to do the impossible. He was expected to build a team that could match the power of Cleveland, Philadelphia, New York, and the other NFL teams. But unfortunately all he had to work with was a collection of washed-up veterans, disgruntled rejects, and inexperienced free agents.

To make matters worse, one of Clem's free agents advertised himself as a former West Virginia end, but after investigating his background, he was exposed as a guy who had been pumping gas since the eighth grade. He never even played *high school* football, much less college football.

Now, don't get me wrong; this is not to say that the 1950 Colts were *entirely* without talent. Many of our better vets from the 1948–49 Colts teams were still with us—guys like Ernie Blandin, Barry French, Bob Nowaskey, and Billy Stone. But gone were Billy Hillenbrand, Charlie O'Rourke, Windell Williams, Hub Bechtol, Racehorse Davis, and Rex Grossman.

That same year I also found myself with another rival. Adrian Burk, a fine quarterback out of Baylor, was Baltimore's No. 1 draft choice that year. We also got Don Colo, a defensive tackle out of Brown University, and Art Donovan. Both ended up staying with the team for many years, and both became two of the game's top performers. Another player who came to us that year was a deadly linebacker from Tulsa University by the name of Hardy Brown.

I remember the Colts being deep in halfbacks from Notre Dame. There was Ernie Zalejski, Frank Spaniel, Bob Livingstone, and Achille Maggioli. We were joined by a great defensive back from Vanderbilt by the name of Herb Rich, and I found a couple of good receivers in Harold Crisler from San Jose State and Jim Owens from Oklahoma.

But even with all these guys, we still couldn't win.

Our first competition, a preseason game, was at home against the Pittsburgh Steelers. We played a good game but as usual found ourselves on the losing end, 30–27. From that point on we continued on a downward spiral; Cleveland creamed us 34–17, the Bears beat us 21–17, San Francisco defeated us 27–14, and the Rams devoured us 70–21.

It was at this time that Abe Warner decided to make an astonishing trade decision. He sent Dick Barwegen to the Chicago

Bears for five players! At that time one for five was unheard of. When questioned about his decision, Warner said, "In my business, five for one has to be a good deal."

The trade proved to be of no help to the Colts. Barwegen was unhappy with his trade and did not want to leave his fish business in Baltimore. Eventually he reported to the Bears. Acquired by the Colts were quarterback George Blanda, halfbacks Bob Perina and Ernie Zalejski, guard Tank Crawford, and end Bob Jensen. But out of the remaining 14 games, we lost 13. Our only win was at home against the other untalented team, the Green Bay Packers, 41–21. Other than that we gave up 462 points for the season. The National Football League stats for 1950 show that most of the records for pass receiving, touchdown passes, and passing yardage were set against Baltimore.

Cardinals quarterback Jim Hardy threw six touchdown passes against us in one game, and end Bob Shaw caught five of them. In that same game the Cards set a record by scoring 48 points in the second half and ended up killing us 55–13. During that ballgame, Clem Crowe, looking around for substitutes, found several Colts players hiding under a blanket. They apparently were not interested in playing. And since it wasn't that cold, I guess they did not want to witness the massacre. In a game against Detroit, end Cloyce Box caught 12 passes in one afternoon and gained 302 yards by himself—another all-time record.

To make matters worse, I was engulfed by my own problems— my throwing arm was extremely sore, I had to compete against George Blanda, and I was in a salary dispute with Abe Warner.

We were playing a preseason game against the New York Yanks when I got cracked on my right arm while throwing a pass. I ended up having to leave the game. A knot the size of a tennis ball developed on my arm and is still there to this day. The doctor told me that I had a spasm in my arm and would not be able to play against the Packers the following week.

The spasm was painful, but it didn't seem bad enough to keep me out of the Green Bay game—but it did—and what bothered me even more was that Blanda got the call to take my place. George had played one year with the Bears and was considered to be an all-around quarterback. He couldn't throw as well as I could, but because he was a great kicker, his worth increased in value. The Packers game was the last preseason show before the final player cuts.

A knot the size of a tennis ball developed on my arm and is still there to this day.

My contract dispute with Abe Warner was eating at me. After reviewing the payroll, Abe had decided that $18,000 was an awful lot of money to be paying a quarterback who had been able to win only one game the year before.

Warner had been after me to sign my contract. My thinking was that Warner would not leave himself without his starting quarterback, but the arrival of Blanda changed the entire picture. Suddenly I realized that I might be expendable. What was worse is that Abe Warner had come to the same conclusion. He told Clem Crowe that I had better sign my contract or I may find myself released from the team.

I had no choice but to concede to Warner. This meeting would cost me money, but I was no longer in a strong bargaining position—at least not with a bad arm and two fine quarterbacks waiting to take over my job.

Abe Warner wasn't a man to waste time babbling in conversation. He quickly began our one-sided negotiations. He said, "I can't afford to pay you $18,000 a year. We are going to lose a lot of ballgames and I'm going to lose a lot of money. I've got to cut down somewhere, and I'm starting with you.

"I want to be fair, so here's what I'll do. I will pay you a base salary of $12,000. If we win five ballgames, I will throw in a $3,000 bonus."

Being only 23 years old and lacking in financial experience, Abe caught me by surprise.

"Can I have some time to think it over?" I stuttered.

"Only until tomorrow," he snapped. "We open the season Sunday, and I want everything settled before then. You've got 24 hours, Tittle!"

That evening I called Cecil Isbell, who was then an assistant coach with the Chicago Cardinals. I told him about my meeting with Warner. He told me that the Cardinals would love to have me (on the premise that Baltimore would give me my release), but they could only offer me $13,000. I was faced with a real dilemma.

I would have loved to play for Isbell again, but Minnette was living in Baltimore and we had had our daughter Diane. I decided to accept Warner's terms.

Although I was the starting quarterback in most of our games that season (splitting the job with Adrian Burk), I didn't throw my first NFL touchdown pass until our sixth game, against San Francisco at Kezar Stadium on October 29, 1950. I came off the bench to replace Burk halfway through the second period. I remember the situation as if it happened yesterday.

It was second down and 15. I threw an incompletion and had a 13-yard completion nullified by an offside penalty. Then I threw a 31-yard touchdown pass to Harold Crisler, the Colts' split end, who ran a post pattern down-and-in. Even though we lost the game 17–14, I had a pretty good day with 18 completions in less than a half for two touchdowns and 230 yards.

Abe ended up in a win-win situation. Baltimore did not win five games—hell, we didn't even win two games. The 1950 Colts had won just once, and that was over the Packers 41–21. By the time we defeated Green Bay, we had lost 19 straight ballgames—a humiliating series of failures that stretched back into 1949.

The end of the 1950 season was also the end of the Baltimore Colts franchise—at least temporarily.

Abe Warner appeared at the NFL owners' meeting the following January pleading for help from the other team owners. No one volunteered.

Warner wanted out, so the league paid him $50,000 for his assets, such as they were. The Colts were officially out of business. All Baltimore players were placed into the 1951 draft—28, including myself, were picked by NFL teams. The others became free agents.

The end of the 1950 season was also the end of the Baltimore Colts franchise—at least temporarily.

All in all, no tears were shed for the passing of the 1950 Baltimore franchise.

13

The Flip of a Coin—
from Baltimore to San Francisco

I BECAME A SAN FRANCISCO 49ER ON THE FLIP OF A COIN. After Baltimore had folded, I found myself exactly where I had been three years before as a green-eared kid out of LSU—in the player draft.

The New York Giants had the bonus pick in 1951—a practice since discontinued—and they selected Kyle Rote, an All-American halfback out of Southern Methodist. It was common knowledge that Rote would be the first man drafted by the pros. The Chicago Bears were next, and they chose quarterback Bob Williams out of Notre Dame. I was beginning to get nervous. Two picks and old Y.A. was still waiting for his turn to come.

With San Francisco, Green Bay, and Washington all having the same dismal 3–9 record the year before, a coin was flipped to determine which club would pick next.

The coin was tossed into the air, and 49ers general manager Lou "Lucky Lou" Spadia called out "Heads!"

I had since moved to Austin and was working in the insurance business. I read about my going to the 49ers in the newspaper the following day. I had figured that one of the clubs would take me, so why not San Francisco.

Heads it was, and Spadia immediately said, "We'll take Y.A. Tittle!"

Soon after, I received a phone call from 49ers owner Tony Morabito. He was coming down to Dallas to meet with me.

Tony, who died of a heart attack during a San Francisco–Chicago Bears home game at Kezar Stadium in 1957, was one of the finest men I have ever met. He was hard-headed but warm-hearted, firm but soft-spoken. He had a great love for the game of professional football.

The son of an Italian immigrant, Tony grew up in the North Beach district of San Francisco—the same area that brought up Joe DiMaggio and many other great baseball players of the time. But Tony's true love had always been football.

After graduating from Santa Clara University, Tony drove a truck but became a professional football fan after fellow alumnus Nello Falaschi, a fullback for the Broncos, began playing for the New York Giants.

In 1941 Tony approached the National Football League and requested a franchise for San Francisco. He was turned down for two reasons: travel to the West Coast was too expensive and the San Francisco area had five major college football teams. He tried once more at the end of World War II but was again turned down by the league.

Morabito wasn't one to give up easily. When he discovered that a Chicago sports editor by the name of Arch Ward was organizing the All-America Football Conference, Tony immediately applied to the new league and San Francisco became a charter member.

Tony knew he would lose money in the beginning, but he believed that San Francisco was a great sports town and was willing to take the gamble.

In 1949 he and his brother Vic bought out their two partners and became sole owners of the 49ers. Tony had so much faith in the team that he mortgaged his home and borrowed $100,000.

He was also very generous to his players. Proof of that was the $20,000 contract he offered to quarterback Frankie Albert—a record salary for that time.

I liked Tony from the moment I met him. He was not only a smart businessman, but he was also fair. I trusted him. A verbal contract for $13,500 was agreed upon. I was anxious to play football on a new team, in a new atmosphere, and with a new administration and coaching staff.

When I returned to Austin I received a phone call Jim Cason, my old LSU sidekick. While I was playing for the Colts, Jim had been with San Francisco. He was glad to once again be playing on the same team with me, and I felt the same way. He told me that Buck Shaw was a fine coach and that the 49ers had a good ballclub.

"Will I get a chance to play out there?" I asked Jim. "Frankie Albert is a San Francisco hero and, frankly, I'm concerned about how much quarterbacking I will do."

"Sure, you'll have a chance to play," he replied encouragingly. "This is a great opportunity for you. Albert's getting old and can't go on forever."

The 49ers training camp was located at Menlo Junior College in Menlo Park, California. When I arrived at camp in July I noticed that Jim Cason was not the only face I knew. Ray Collins, the big tackle from LSU, and linebacker Hardy Brown, who had played with me for a year with the Colts, were also there.

San Francisco had faired well in the 1951 draft. Joe Arenas came in with me that year as did Pete Schabarum, Rex Berry, Jim Monachino, Bill Jessup, and other top ballplayers.

Training camp under Buck Shaw was different from anything I had ever experienced as a pro. With the exception of the 1950 season—when the 49ers held a bleak 3–9 record, San Francisco had been a winning team. True, they had never won a league championship, but they were always close behind those great Cleveland teams. The 49ers demonstrated a winning spirit, Buck Shaw gave the team confidence, and Frankie Albert recorded victories.

Coach Shaw coached his ballclub with kid gloves. He was truly a gentleman—dapper, polished, and soft-spoken. His roughest language consisted of, "Damn it to hell!" But when those words were spoken, players who were not giving it their all quickly began to do so.

Shaw had a casual approach to coaching. He was well organized and commanded respect but never resorted to the driving, sweating, and cursing tactics that other coaches used. He had the ability of getting his ballplayers to rise to the occasion without painful tongue-lashings, punishing wind sprints, or annoying bed checks. He created an atmosphere of relaxation, but nobody ever took advantage of Buck. He may not have always had the best players in the league, but he achieved maximum results with the men that he had.

I always felt that my best years as a quarterback and my effectiveness as a football player were under the regime of Buck Shaw (1951–1954). After Buck left San Francisco, the coaching style became rigid, disciplined, and controlled. I missed him very much.

How a coach coaches is not for me to say. He has to run his ballclub the way he sees fit. Paul Brown, a strong, stern personality, was a winning coach at Cleveland, but so was Buck Shaw— first at Santa Clara where his teams won in the Sugar Bowl, then in San Francisco, and later with the Eagles in Philadelphia.

In 1961 Buck did a great coaching job with the Eagles. He had a quarterback by the name of Norm Van Brocklin and not much else, but he won the Eastern title and beat the Green Bay Packers 17–13 for the world championship.

Buck Shaw did as much for my psychological approach to football as Cecil Isbell did for my confidence in my passing game. He treated me as a man and as a pro. There was nothing I wanted more to do than to win for him.

After Buck left San Francisco, the coaching style became rigid, disciplined, and controlled. I missed him very much.

14

Quarterback Frankie Albert

NO PLAYER TYPIFIED THE SAN FRANCISCO 49ERS MORE THAN quarterback Frankie Albert.

The success of the team in those early years was founded on Tony Morabito's dollars and faith, on Buck Shaw's organizational ability, and, perhaps more than anything else, on Frankie Albert's dramatic plays and fan appeal. Frankie was a leader on the field and an inspiration to the team.

My first impression of Albert in 1951 was that he was far more polished than the other ballplayers I had known. He was older than the rest of us and showed it in his self-confidence and maturity. On away trips, Frankie would sit with the sportswriters and the coaches while the rest of us played cards and goofed off. He carried with him an air of poise and articulation, unlike the others.

I never knew how he really felt about me, but I can tell you one thing: he never went out of his way to further my development as a quarterback. The only way I could learn from Albert was by studying him in action from the sideline.

What struck me most about him was his approach to the game. He had fun playing the game and at the same time made it fun for us. He was the guy who could always be expected to do the unexpected, especially during practice.

For instance Frankie might just keep the ball on a bootleg when everyone expected him to do something else. He would catch everyone off guard by handing the ball to a lineman or maybe to a guy who was just standing there watching the play. It broke the monotony of the practice.

When he wasn't in the huddle Albert would be over on the far sideline punting and throwing the ball to a bunch of kids who were taking in the practice.

Players were not allowed to smoke on the field during practice. That rule didn't apply to Buck Shaw. He had a habit of flipping his cigarette over his shoulder when he was finished with it. Frankie would then sneak up behind him, take a couple of forbidden puffs off the cigarette, then return back to the huddle. Albert may have clowned around a bit, but he knew where to draw the line when it came to Coach Shaw.

Off the field, Frankie didn't let anyone get too close to him. I never felt as though he was "one of the guys."

One of the players on our team was a big tackle from the University of Minnesota by the name of Leo "Nomo" Nomellini. Nomellini's hero was Bronko Nagurski, one of the game's all-time great fullbacks. Even though Leo was an All-Pro tackle, he always wished he could have been another Nagurski. Frankie knew this. During practice and in some of our scrimmages, Albert would come into the huddle and say, "Well, okay, let's run a 31 Wedge. Nomo, you get back here and play fullback."

Leo would drop back from his tackle spot into halfback Johnny Strzykalski's spot and Johnny would

Frankie would then sneak up behind him, take a couple of forbidden puffs off the cigarette, then return back to the huddle.

fill in for Leo. Nomellini really enjoyed the switch, but I'm not so sure that Strzykalski shared his same feelings.

Leo played the position like a charging elephant, and when Albert would hand him the ball he would run up through the middle on a 31 Wedge. The defense would kick the hell out of him, but Leo loved it.

Frankie also did this in regular games. Whenever we had a big lead in the final period, he would use a play called "31 Nomo." Leo would get into the fullback position, prance his legs up and down, and snort a few times. Then Frankie would call the signals, "Hut-one…hut-two," and he would hand off the ball to Leo.

Everyone would holler, "Attaboy, Leo, you killed 'em that time!"

Most times Nomellini only gained a yard or two, but we made it sound like he was ripping up the defense.

While in the huddle, Albert would look at Leo and say, "Damn! You're really cracking that line today, Leo. I'll tell you what we're going to do. We're going to pound you in there a few more times to soften them up, then we'll shoot Cason or Strzykalski to the outside." Leo couldn't be happier.

31 Nomo was a great play. It may not have gotten us much yardage, but it made the 49ers a better team just the same.

Frankie had other ways of keeping everyone guessing. One of them was throwing passes for extra points. The fact that we had a great place kicker in Gordy Soltau didn't matter to Albert. He would hold the ball for Soltau on the conversion, then once the ball was hiked, Frankie would stand up and lob it to a defensive end who would run it in for the extra point.

It never made much sense to me. After all, Gordy was a sure thing for the extra point—the defensive end wasn't. Frankie knew this, but it was his way of having fun and enjoying the game.

Albert had alternate reasons for his showmanship. Those lob passes for the extra point rubbed salt into the wounded pride of the other team. It was bad enough to be scored upon, but to then have this little left-hander toss the ball in for the extra point was downright humiliating. Frankie knew this and used his trickery to his full advantage.

I have been called a good bootlegger in my time, but I couldn't carry Albert's helmet when it came to bootlegging the football. He was truly a master of the game. (Author's note: A bootleg is an offensive play where the quarterback fakes a handoff to a running back going one direction while he goes the opposite direction to run or pass.)

The bootleg was a psychological weapon in Albert's arsenal. The fact that you make five yards on a run or that you can complete a 10-yard pass to Billy Wilson when you just as easily could have dropped back and hit him on the hook pattern will most likely not confuse a defense. But if the quarterback can roll out and throw one in the opposite direction, he can ruin an opposing team's morale.

Improvisation was Frankie's middle name. He would make up plays any time, any place. It was as if he pulled them out of the air. Most quarterbacks couldn't get away with this, but Albert could. He was an instinctive quarterback who had an incredible feel for the game. He did things that no one else could.

In August 1952 the 49ers played a preseason game against the Chicago Cardinals. Hugh McElhenny made his pro debut in that game. In the huddle Albert turned to Mac and said, "I'm going to fake to Perry up the middle. I want you to delay for one count and then start swinging around the end. I'll pitch it out to you."

"What play is that?" asked McElhenny.

"It's no play," snapped Albert. "Just do what I tell you."

"Okay," said Mac.

Hugh took off for the right sideline as Albert made his fake to Perry. The Cardinals defenders were frozen for a split second as Perry crashed into the line. That instant was all Frankie needed as he turned and lateraled the ball to Mac in the flat. Hugh went 66 yards for the touchdown. The defense never saw him.

I have been called a good bootlegger in my time, but I couldn't carry Albert's helmet when it came to bootlegging the football.

During a game against the Yankees, a group of photographers behind the end zone shouted to Albert that they had been unable to get any good close-up action shots.

"Stay right where you are, fellas." Frankie answered, not caring whether or not the Yankees heard him. "I'll pitch out to Strzykalski, and he'll come right at you."

The play developed just as Albert had described it. The San Francisco line opened up a hole, Strzykalski went through for the score, and the photographers had their picture.

Frankie Albert led the 49ers with flair of arrogance that could almost be construed as insulting to his opponents. He may not have been a great forward passer—he threw a left-handed ball that wobbled all over the place—but his imagination, great reflexes, flamboyance for the unexpected, and nerves of steel made him a dangerous quarterback.

There has never been a better ball handler in professional football than Albert. Maybe Eddie LeBaron came close, but in my opinion Frankie was still the best. He could shuffle the ball in the backfield and make it disappear. I recall that even when looking at our game films in slow motion that it was sometimes difficult to locate the ball when Albert was working his sleight-of-hand magic.

Whenever I consider my status in professional football, I can't help but think that Cecil Isbell and Frankie Albert, each in their own way, made the most important contributions to my early development. Isbell gave me the confidence in my ability to throw the football—to pick my man and to hit him between the eyes. Albert taught me the nuances and refinements of quarterbacking—not to mention the bootleg play.

15

I Came to San Francisco to Play

WHEN I CAME TO SAN FRANCISCO IN 1951, FRANKIE ALBERT was their No. 1 quarterback and in his sixth season. It was going to take a lot for me to take over the No. 1 spot. I knew that I was a better passer than Albert, but he was a far superior quarterback in every other aspect of the position, including the most important: he knew how to win games.

When I signed with Tony Morabito it was with the intent that I would play—not ride the bench until Albert decided to retire.

"You'll get your chance," Tony had said, and his word was good enough for me.

I enjoyed training at Menlo Park. The atmosphere was relaxed—not like the other pro camps I had attended in the past. Buck Shaw believed in informality. The first day at practice he walked on to the field and said, "Okay, boys, you all start running some plays."

Heck, we hadn't even learned any plays yet.

Then he said, "You older guys show these new fellows some plays."

Next thing we knew, Albert and fullbacks Norm Standlee and Johnny Strzykalski and the rest of the guys got up there and started running plays. Frankie pretty much ran the show by himself after Shaw got things under way. He made up the plays as he went along. No one had so much as seen a 49ers playbook, but I got the impression we didn't need one as long as Frankie was in charge of things. He never had any trouble. If he couldn't remember a play, he simply invented one. The veterans were so used to his off-the-cuff improvising that they fell right into line.

> *If he couldn't remember a play, he simply invented one.*

Frankie would stick his head in the huddle and say, "Everybody zone, and we'll pitch out to you, Strzykalski." The play would be run as if they had practiced it a thousand times before. It was really something to see.

This is not to say that Coach Shaw was not well organized—quite the contrary. His record will attest to that. He was a winning coach who coached his way. His approach may have been different, but it was successful.

Football in 1951 was much different than it is today. That's why Buck was able to coach the way he did. Back then we didn't study two sets of game films before each game. We never studied automatics; hell, we didn't even have automatics back then. Preparation for a game then compared to the preparation it takes to play in today's game is like night and day.

The job of the quarterback was much easier and simpler then because the "age of the specialist" had yet to be invented. We did not have to face the great defensive stars of today who play in the National Football League. In those days the average lifespan of a pro was two or three years. Today quarterbacks have to contend with defensive specialists—those who have 10 years or more of experience. A defensive cornerback like Ronnie Lott, a linebacker like Dave Wilcox, or an end like Fred Dean all have size, speed, and great experience. They are hard to beat. All we had in 1951 was a 5-3-2-1 defense, slant left, slant right, and maybe a few Red Dogs. (Author's note: A Red Dog is a defensive strategy in which a linebacker or defensive back vacates his normal responsibilities in order to pressure the quarterback. The object of a Red Dog is to tackle the quarterback behind the line of scrimmage or force the quarterback to hurry his pass. Today it is simply known as "blitzing.") That was it. There was no need for detailed preparations. Playing was simple, and so was coaching.

Throughout training camp at Menlo that summer I looked better than Albert in practice. As usual, he passed poorly and I passed well. I was throwing nice tight spirals while Frankie was throwing the ball end over end. But throwing spirals wasn't going to land me the starting position. I would have to prove that I could win before San Francisco considered me anything more than a bald-headed guy from Baltimore.

My chance to prove what I could do was delayed due to a muscle pull that I received during the second week of training camp. I was sidelined for the next two games. In the meantime Frankie whipped the Redskins 45–14 in the preseason opener at home but lost to Chicago the following week, 24–7. Then it was my turn.

My injury had healed well, and the 49ers were on their way to meet the Pittsburgh Steelers the following week in Syracuse, New York.

I felt ready; at least I thought I was. We made the trip to Syracuse by train. What a long ride! The bouncing up and down in the sleeper car caused my bursitis to act up. I had stabbing pains in my right shoulder and couldn't even carry my suitcase

My chance to prove what I could do was delayed due to a muscle pull that I received during the second week of training camp.

95

off the train. *Damn it,* I thought. *How am I going to throw the ball tomorrow night?*

I was debating whether or not I should tell Coach Shaw about my shoulder. The team knew nothing of my bursitis, and I wanted it to stay that way. I had just come off the injured list and had no desire to be placed back on it—not with my first opportunity to start just a day away. How could I explain the bursitis? The guys would begin to think that I was a hypochondriac.

These thoughts were running through my mind when fate intervened. A torrential rainstorm hit Syracuse. It was the heaviest rain to ever hit the city. The streets were flooded, power lines came down, and Syracuse was at a standstill. The storm was so violent that the game was postponed. That is the only time I can remember a football game being cancelled on account of rain— and it was also the break I was looking for. My arm would now get an extra day's rest.

The following day most of the guys hung around the hotel playing cards, but not me. I paid a visit to the doctor who was with the Syracuse International League baseball team. I don't remember how I got his name and number, but I didn't want to go to the 49ers' trainer, Pop Kleckner. I didn't want him to know about my shoulder. He had just taken care of my muscle pull, and I didn't want to look like I was a chronic injury candidate.

The Syracuse doctor treated my shoulder with electrical-impulse treatments and an injection of cortisone. I repeated the treatment the following day, and by game time my shoulder was well enough to make it through. I was well aware of the fact that I wouldn't be throwing the ball too well but would be able to bluff my way through when called upon by Coach Shaw.

Frankie started the game, and then I came in during the second half. I managed to play well enough without anyone noticing my sore shoulder, and with the majority of the help from Albert we beat the Steelers 44–17.

The 1950 season was not a good one. Our record was a disappointing 3–9, but in 1951 the 49ers were a good football team. Not only did we have a good draft that year, but I had one of the greatest ends I have ever seen in Billy Wilson. We finished the season with a 7–6–1 record—a big improvement over the last season.

When the regular season had started, Albert was the starting quarterback, which was to be expected. We won the opener by upsetting Cleveland 24–10. I didn't get a chance to play in that game, but I didn't mind. Frankie had six years on me, and more importantly he had the confidence of the players. I was sure that someday I would be a better quarterback than Frankie, but it would take time and patience.

Albert was an off-the-cuff quarterback, and I knew it would be wrong for me to try and adapt my style of play to his. Also Frankie was left-handed and did everything opposite of what I did. But what I did learn from him was his approach to the game. He was not afraid to take chances, and he thrived on pressure. He enjoyed playing football and made the game enjoyable for his team—even when we were playing for big money.

In our opening game against Cleveland, Frankie had hurt his shoulder and could barely throw the ball. Coach Shaw didn't have enough faith in me to call the plays because I was still trying to learn their offense. So Albert continued to play, bad shoulder and all. We lost the next game to Philadelphia by a score of 24–14 and came home from a road trip three weeks later with a 2–2 record.

I was still gathering splinters on the bench when San Francisco played Los Angeles in the fifth game of the season. The 1951 Rams were a great team. They were loaded with speed and power

I was still gathering splinters on the bench when San Francisco played Los Angeles in the fifth game of the season.

and had great passers in Bob Waterfield and Norm "the Dutchman" Van Brocklin. Los Angeles also had three of the best receivers in pro football—Elroy "Crazylegs" Hirsch, Tom Fears, and Bob Boyd. But that particular day, we were better than them. Frankie was tremendous and drove the Rams crazy with his plays. The defense was right on as it picked off six Rams passes. Visco Grgich and Leo Nomellini made life miserable for Waterfield and Van Brocklin—so miserable that Van Brocklin hit his boiling point and challenged Grgich to a fight after the game. Visco declined the invitation, telling the Dutchman that he was sorry, but he was a coward. We beat them 44–17.

A week later Los Angeles returned the favor by beating us 23–16 on three field goals by Waterfield. That left us with a 3–3 record when the New York Yanks came to Kezar Stadium.

The New York game was the turning point in my career as a 49er. The Yanks were basically a weak ballclub, but not that day. By the fourth quarter they were ahead 14–12. That's when Shaw put me in the game. I had no alternative but to throw the ball and score quickly because time was running out.

In the huddle I looked at Gordy Soltau, our left end and asked him, "Can you beat your man to the inside?"

"I'll try," he said.

"Okay, then, the snap number is on three. Let's pull this one out!"

As I dropped back to throw, the Yanks defense blitzed, and they broke through my blockers. It would have been suicide to have stood my ground, so I scrambled out to the right. I was able to get away from two tacklers and looked downfield for Soltau. There he was—wide open and cutting across the middle of the field. I threw a pass, maybe 35 yards or more toward Gordy. Just as I released the ball I got the hell knocked out of me. I was flipped clean over backwards. As I hit the ground I heard the crowd cheering. We had scored!

"Nice going, Gordy," I said as I got back on my feet.

But when I got to the sideline, everyone was congratulating and shaking hands with our flanker back, Pete Schabarum.

"What's going on?" I asked Jim Cason, who had been sitting on the bench.

"You just won the ballgame for us, that's what," he said.

"Yeah, I know, but why is everyone congratulating Schabarum?"

"Because he is the one who caught your pass," said Jimmy.

It was then that I had realized that I had missed Soltau by a good two yards and the ball landed in Schabarum's hands. He had caught it on a dead run and ran it right into the end zone for the score and the game!

After the game the sportswriters said it was the prettiest pass ever thrown in Kezar Stadium. Even though I was embarrassed, I was not embarrassed enough to tell them that my real target was Soltau and not Schabarum. Hell, I didn't even know where Pete was when I released the ball!

This was not my first touchdown pass for San Francisco, but it was my biggest. It won the game for us, and I wanted this win for the team. I wanted to win for the players just as Frankie had won for the past six years.

My lucky touchdown pass to Pete also aroused controversy in the papers. Several writers asked, "Why doesn't Buck Shaw use Tittle more?" A quarterback controversy was born.

> *My lucky touchdown pass to Pete also aroused controversy in the papers.*

Frankie never mentioned whether or not it bothered him. We were still not close friends and didn't have much to say to one another.

The one person the Tittle-Albert controversy did bother was Buck Shaw. He told one of the San Francisco writers, "I knew that inevitably we were going to get into this squeeze. It's the same thing in Los Angeles, where they have Waterfield and Van Brocklin. One or the other is always on the pan with the fans and the press. That, or the coaches are."

When we played the Yanks a second time, New York was the one who would enjoy their day in the sun. Two weeks after we had played them at Kezar Stadium, we flew east to meet them in New York. Again, Coach Shaw sent me in for Albert, this time with the score tied at 10–10 with two minutes left on the clock. We marched down the field, and it seemed like we were going in for the score. I completed a pass to Soltau on the Yanks' 15-yard line, which would have been good range for a field-goal try. But Gordy lateraled the ball to Johnny Strzykalski as he was being tackled, and he fumbled the ball. The Yanks recovered and ran out the clock.

After the game I flung my helmet on the floor of the Yankee Stadium dressing room. I slumped down on a stool and was thoroughly disappointed at having to settle for a tie with a ballclub we should have easily beaten.

If you look back at the Western Division standings for 1951, you will see that San Francisco had a good chance to win the title. At least we did until the Yanks tied us in New York. That field goal Soltau lateraled away would have made us a contender.

I was sitting in the locker room cursing to myself and thinking about the lost field goal when a writer from the *San Francisco Chronicle* walked up.

"Well, Y.A., you almost did it again."

Now this comment came *immediately* after the game. We didn't have the 10-minute cooling-off period that they have today. I was still angry about the loss.

"Well, dammit," I snorted. "I can't do it every week with two minutes left in the game!"

The minute the words left my mouth I knew I shouldn't have said them. They were uttered under emotional stress, but it was too late—the damage had been done.

Without a word, the writer walked away. With another week on the road I was unaware of the repercussions my untimely statement created back in San Francisco.

The headlines read, "Tittle Criticizes Shaw for Lack of Play!" The letters were set in the largest type the *Chronicle* could find.

The story under the headline was even more inflammatory. It quoted me as saying, "This is a passing game and not a running game," implying that I was criticizing Buck Shaw's game plan and Frankie Albert's field strategy. They put other words in my mouth too...words I never said. The only thing I had said, regrettably, was that I couldn't win every week with two minutes to go. Like many other professional football players, I learned the hard way to weigh my words carefully with members of the press.

The following week we played Detroit, and I came back again to win the ballgame for San Francisco, 20–10. I really don't like to say that "I" won the game, because I didn't win it alone. The rest of the team was just as much a part of the win as I was. But I did get more playing time, and my passing gave us the winning points in the second half.

A quarterback is evaluated by how many games he wins. And I was beginning to win ballgames for the 49ers.

Frankie Albert was still the first-string quarterback, and Buck Shaw never led me to believe any differently. But I knew I was making headway.

By the time we returned to San Francisco, I was still unaware of the sensation my Yankee Stadium outburst had caused at home. Once Coach Shaw heard about it, he summoned me to his office.

"Sit down, Y.A.," he said. "There is something we've got to talk about."

I immediately got the sense that this meeting was not going to be good.

"Did you see this article?" he asked, holding a copy of the *Chronicle* in front of me.

"No," I replied.

Then he asked, "Did you make this statement?"

I hastily read the beginning of the story and said, "Well, yes, Buck, but I didn't make these other statements about 'this is a passing game' and 'I believe you should throw the ball more' and that 'you can't play pro teams and score 10 points and expect to win.' I never said any of those things."

Coach's expression remained unchanged.

"You know, Y.A., this makes me look awful bad, and it's not good for our ballclub, either."

Buck was right, and I was wrong. I apologized even though I felt then, as I do now, that the *Chronicle* story was unfair and inaccurate. I felt deeply embarrassed and was sorry for Coach. He had always treated me fairly, and it was not my intention to put him on the spot.

Since that fateful day at Yankee Stadium in 1951, I have kept my guard up with sportswriters. Many of them are good people, but there are those who are out for sensationalism who can ruin a ballplayer's career.

Buck never again mentioned the incident, and the minute we walked out the door, it was a closed issue. I, too, put it out of my mind and concentrated on our last two games against the Packers and the Lions.

Since that fateful day at Yankee Stadium in 1951, I have kept my guard up with sportswriters.

In the game against Green Bay, Frankie and I split the quarterbacking position. We won the ballgame 31–19.

Detroit marched into Kezar Stadium needing only a victory over the 49ers to clinch the NFL Western Division title. The Lions had a 7–3–1 record while the Rams held on to a 7–4 record. Our record was 6–4–1 going into the final game of the 1951 regular season.

Frankie started the game, but Coach Shaw put me in much earlier than usual, and I ended up playing the majority of the game.

With four minutes left in the game, we were behind 17–14, but Joe Arenas caught a Detroit punt and ran 51 yards to the 9-yard line. With that, I ran in the winning touchdown on a bootleg play with a minute to go on the clock. I can still remember that play as if it were executed yesterday. I faked to Joe Perry over the middle and then to John Strzykalski on a slant. The Detroit linebackers took the second fake. They didn't even see me hide the ball on my hip and go into the end zone standing up.

As I walked off the field in jubilation, Lions halfback Hunchy Hoernschemeyer was enraged and directed a derogatory statement toward me. The 49ers had just cost Hoernschemeyer and his Lions teammates a bundle of playoff money.

Even though the 1951 49ers team did not finish first, it was a fine football team that carried with it a great deal of spirit and pride. Our backfield of Joe Perry, Johnny Strzykalski, and Joe Arenas was as good as any in the league.

Arenas was the fighting spirit of the 1951 team. He epitomized the hustle and aggressiveness of the entire squad. A small halfback out of Omaha, Joe was an unheralded draft choice and wasn't given much of a chance at winning the starting left halfback position. But Joe had different ideas.

During our first day in training camp, Albert called the squad together and said, "Let's line up out there and run some plays."

Norm Standlee filled in at the fullback position, Johnny Strzykalski was at halfback, Bill Johnson was at center, and Bruno Banducci made his way to the line. But before any of the other veterans could make a move, Arenas filled in at the left halfback position. Rookies aren't supposed to take such liberties, but there he was, big as life. Everyone looked at everyone else in amazement. The same question was going through everyone's mind: *Who the hell does this little guy think he is?*

Joe wasn't exactly popular with the veterans in the beginning. As a matter of fact, there were a few guys who downright hated his guts. He was brash and cocky, but it was this arrogance and aggressiveness that got him the starting job. From that day forward Joe never lost the left halfback position. His passion for winning and his team spirit caught on with the rest of the squad.

Frankie Albert and Joe Arenas were quite a pair in 1951!

16

Hardy Brown: The Toughest Football Player I Ever Met

POUND FOR POUND, INCH FOR INCH, THE TOUGHEST FOOTBALL player I ever met was my 49ers roommate Hardy Brown. He was so tough he was damned near illegal!

Hardy was a linebacker and played the position with so much force that he put fear in rival ball carriers. He was known for his numbing shoulder tackle, which was usually aimed at the head of his opponent. When Hardy hit them, they stayed on the ground until they were carried away on a stretcher.

From 1951 through 1955 Hardy Brown was the punisher of professional football. I played with him for five years and saw him do things that were almost unbelievable.

While playing the Washington Redskins in 1951, I watched him knock out the entire starting backfield, leaving only Harry Gilmer, the Redskins' quarterback, in one piece. When I say "knocked out," I mean that literally!

Against the Rams that same year, Hardy caught halfback Glenn Davis coming through a hole in the line and hit him so hard in the head that the ligaments were torn in Glenn's knees. Davis was never the same again and quit football shortly thereafter.

Hardy always played tough, but he seemed to be at his best when the 49ers were playing our rivals, the Rams. On the final

Against the Rams that same year, Hardy caught halfback Glenn Davis coming through a hole in the line and hit him so hard in the head that the ligaments were torn in Glenn's knees.

play of a San Francisco–Los Angeles game at the LA Coliseum, running back Dick Hoerner carried for the Rams and met Brown head-on at the line of scrimmage. The gun sounded as they crashed to the ground. Both teams then left the field and entered their respective locker rooms. The Rams soon discovered that one of their players was missing—Dick Hoerner. When they went outside to the field, they found Dick just getting to his feet. He had been knocked cold for at least 15 minutes, and Hardy had left him for dead right on the 3-yard line!

There were a lot of players in the NFL who were out for Hardy Brown—especially those from the Rams. Rumor had it that Los Angeles had a pool set up to pay the fine of any man who put Hardy out of commission. They never did.

The only time I ever saw Brown get hurt was when he slammed into a Detroit runner. He hit him so hard that the player bounced off the ground, catching Hardy under the chin. The cut required six stitches, but he was back in the game in a matter of minutes. Hardy could not only dish it out, but he could also take it.

That shoulder tackle of his was really something to see. I was just glad that he was a teammate of mine on both my Baltimore and 49ers teams. I'm thankful that I never had to play against him.

Hardy never used his arms to tackle. He got down in a crouch, like a panther waiting to spring on his prey, and when the runner got close enough Hardy would come up under him and drive his shoulder toward the ball carrier's head. His timing was perfect. When he connected with that shoulder block, their heads would snap back and they would drop in their tracks. To this day

I never saw a football player who could take out an opponent like Hardy Brown.

I remember one game in particular when we were playing the Steelers at Kezar Stadium during the 1951 season. Pittsburgh had a small but tough halfback named Joe Geri. He and Hardy went at each other all afternoon. In the fourth quarter, Brown decided to end the contest. The play was a handoff to Geri. As Joe came running up the field, Hardy threw a shoulder into Geri. The hit was so incredibly hard that Brown popped Joe's eyeball clean out of the socket! It was literally hanging down on his cheek!

The hit was so incredibly hard that Brown popped Joe's eyeball clean out of the socket! It was literally hanging down on his cheek!

Rival clubs began to think that Hardy was deliberately trying to injure or maim his opponents. They sent officials into the San Francisco dressing room to check Hardy's shoulder pads—they didn't believe he could do so much damage with just regulation gear. They never found anything.

Hardy was called everything from a dirty player to a hatchet man, but nothing seemed to bother Brown. I always felt that he enjoyed being tagged as a bad guy.

One day I said to him, "Hardy, I think you'd pop that shoulder into your own mother."

He replied with, "Not unless she had a football under her arm, Y.A."

Somehow I felt he wasn't kidding.

Whether those shoulder hits were legal or not, Hardy Brown gave the 1951 San Francisco team a real lift. That year Hardy knocked out 21 opponents!

As my roommate, he was quiet and reserved. I used to watch him sitting there reading a book and wonder how he could be so devastating in a pair of shoulder pads.

I kidded him once by saying, "There are times, Hardy, when I actually feel you are human."

"Just try and run past me with a football, and you'll see how human I am," he shot back.

Once again, I am sure he was joking, but just the same, there was a glint in his blue eyes that gave me a chill. I do believe Hardy would have dropped me right there in the dorm had I taken him up on his gesture.

Coach Buck Shaw knew how tough Hardy was and refused to allow him to take part in our scrimmages and intrasquad games!

As a quarterback who sometimes found himself across the line from Hardy, I emphatically endorsed this ban—as did the rest of the team. We all loved Hardy but not enough to let him knock our heads off in practice!

Hardy really resented this arrangement, but there was no other way to deal with the situation. He never learned how to tackle properly, and he couldn't lock his arms around the ball carrier's legs in a legal style of tackling. All he wanted to do was throw a shoulder block into somebody's face—and those were the days before face masks!

But in all fairness, Brown was the ideal middle linebacker in the San Francisco 5-3 defense because his duties were easy. His main job was plugging holes when the guard pulled. Most of his tackles were made in the middle of the line at point-blank range. When the 4-3 defense came along, Hardy was through. It was difficult for him to play the middle spot in the 4-3 because he was forced to pursue his opponent in the open field and make his tackles on the run—something he had never been required to do in the past. He turned out to be a poor tackler and missed his opponent too often. But mind you, when he did hit his man, it hurt clear up to the last row of seats.

Hardy and I had played together in both Baltimore and with the 49ers and had been close friends since 1950, and it was therefore ironic and unfortunate that I would be the one responsible for Hardy being cut from the team. Well, maybe I was not entirely responsible for his release, but I felt that I was a part of it just the same.

In 1956 Hardy was on a fine line of being cut by Frankie Albert, who was then the 49ers' head coach. Brown was not the player he had once been and was financially in bad shape. Everyone liked Hardy and didn't want to see him go, but Frankie and the rest of his coaching staff were giving him his final chance with the squad.

That Saturday afternoon we were having a big scrimmage game. I knew this would be the competition that would either make or break Hardy. I decided to help him out.

The morning of the scrimmage I confronted Hardy and suggested we make him look good in the practice.

"How?" he asked.

"I've devised a set of signals that will tip you off where the play is going," I answered, not without a feeling of shame.

"That's not right," protested Hardy.

"I know, but it won't hurt anybody, and it might make you look good in front of Albert. He's getting ready to drop you, Hardy."

Hardy was hesitant about going along with my plan. It was against his nature and against mine too, but it was the only way to save his job.

Finally he said, "Okay, what do I do?"

"Just watch me when the offense comes out of the huddle."

"What should I be looking for?" Brown asked, scratching his head.

"If it's going to be a pass, I'll rub my hands together."

Hardy nodded.

My intentions were not to throw the ball to Hardy, but at least he would have the chance to drop back and look good covering his pass zone. Pass coverage was never one of his strong points, and I knew that the coaches would be watching him closely.

"Now if we are going to run the ball around right end, I'll come up to the line and raise my right arm. If the play is going left, I'll put my left arm up in the air. I will keep my hands together if the play goes up the middle."

"Won't that be too obvious?" asked Hardy with a worried look on his face.

"Maybe, but we can't worry about that now."

My plan was executed to the letter, and Hardy looked great. He was slamming into the holes, tackling ball carriers, and dropping back and covering passes with skill and expertise.

Everything was going well until Albert decided to send in Earl Morrall to replace me at quarterback. Hardy's face was one of sheer panic. He knew that Morrall was not part of the plan to save his job.

Frankie had decided to send the plays in from the sideline, as Paul Brown did at Cleveland, instead of letting Morrall call his own plays.

As Frankie got up there on the sideline, kneeling on one knee, I was right behind him. I made it look as though I was very interested in the scrimmage, but what I was really doing was listening in on the play-calling and signaling the plays to Hardy.

Hardy's face was one of sheer panic.

It worked for a while, and Hardy was looking great. Twice he tackled the runner for big losses and two or three times he knocked down passes in the secondary. Frankie's interest grew—then trouble hit.

110

When I first began signaling from the sideline, the ball was on the 50-yard line and Hardy was looking at me. In other words I was in front of him and he could glance across the line and see my play-calling. But all of a sudden Albert ordered the offense and defense to change sides. This caused Hardy to turn and look back over his shoulder in order to see me. The change in direction had confused Hardy. When I raised my right arm to tip off a play going right, he took a quick look at me and ran to the left—away from the play. He didn't know whether right meant right or left. Hardy got worse with each play. If the play went right, he went left and vice versa. It was awful.

When the scrimmage was over, so was Hardy's professional football career. The 49ers cut him.

17

A Quarterback Controversy

BY THE START OF THE 1952 TRAINING-CAMP SEASON, the San Francisco quarterback controversy had become a real headache for Buck Shaw.

The 49ers fans were divided, half insisting that Albert be the No. 1 quarterback and the other half insisting that Shaw give me more playing time. The local media had a field day with this. Training camp opened under unfavorable conditions, and nobody seemed to know who was going to play where.

The controversy was solved when Shaw decided to implement a rotation plan. One week Frankie would start and play the first and third quarters and I would come into the game in the second and fourth quarters. The following week the rotation would reverse. Buck made it very clear to the team that, win or lose, that was the way it was going to be.

Frankie was a better all-around quarterback, but that didn't prevent me from saying "Hot damn" to myself when Coach Shaw announced his decision. It looked like I was finally going to get my chance to throw the football.

Albert and I were still not close, and I didn't know how he felt about the split arrangement that Buck figured would get the wolves off his back. He never confided in me nor I in him. There was always an age and maturity barrier between us, and now a complicated, competitive angle was added that forced the wedge even deeper into our relationship.

But whatever Frankie's personal feelings were, he was first and foremost a team player and never gave any sign that the situation bothered him. He played brilliantly during the early part of the '52 season as we piled up five straight victories. We defeated Detroit 17–13, Dallas 37–14, Detroit again—in one of the most memorable games I ever played in—a shutout of 28–0, Chicago 40–16, and Dallas again, 48–21.

The city of San Francisco was overjoyed with its team when we returned from our road trip leading the NFL's Western Division with a 5–0 record. Even the fans' controversy about Frankie and me united in the common cause: a championship for the Bay Area and for Tony and Vic Morabito and Coach Shaw.

This 1952 49ers team was a sound and polished ballclub. Even with Frankie and me trading the quarterback position every 15 minutes, the offense had no trouble scoring. McElhenny was running wild and scoring at will, and our defense had Hardy Brown (who was in his prime) plus linebackers Norm Standlee and Don Burke, ends Ed Henke and Charlie Powell, and Jim Cason and Lowell Wagner in the secondary.

One of my most memorable games was the fourth game of the '52 season against the Lions, where we shut them out 28–0. The defense played brilliantly. The Lions didn't get their initial first down until the end of the fourth quarter. Charlie Powell, a rookie end who weighed in at only 215 pounds, got the starting job that day. Injuries had plagued the team, and our roster was down to only 28 available men. During the warm-up, line coach Phil Bengston pulled Charlie aside and told him he would open at defensive end.

"You only have to remember one thing, Charlie. Just drive in and rush Bobby Layne as hard and as often as you can," said Bengston.

"Which one is he?" asked the naïve 19-year-old Powell.

"He'll be the guy throwing the ball," said Phil. "That's all you need to know. Now go after him!"

From that point on, Charlie was all over Layne. He draped himself around Bobby's neck on nearly every play. Layne was one of the league's all-time great passers, but not that day. He didn't complete a pass until the fourth quarter. When Charlie got through with him, Bobby was black and blue and sore as hell.

Even though we beat Detroit twice that year, they still managed to win the Western Division championship with a 9–3 record. But to our efforts, the Lions were only able to score three points in two games—thanks to our tremendous defense.

By the time we met the Chicago Bears on November 2 at Kezar Stadium, things were looking pretty good for the 49ers. With a 5–0 record, the division title would be that much closer with a second defeat over the Bears.

But fate was not on our side, and our entire season took a turn for the worse on one single play.

We were leading the Bears 17–10 in the fourth quarter. With fourth down and two yards to go on the San Francisco 32, Albert dropped back to punt. Frankie was pretty consistent in punting, so we figured that the ball would land somewhere between the Chicago 20- or 30-yard line. But Albert had other plans.

Frankie saw daylight between a Bears tackle and the end, so instead of punting, he made a run for it. It was the kind of gamble he had executed successfully in the past, but this time the hole closed up

But fate was not on our side, and our entire season took a turn for the worse on one single play.

immediately. Ed Sprinkle, a Chicago end who knew that Frankie liked to run from a punt formation, hit him short of the first down. A loud groan from the fans resonated throughout the stadium. They had just witnessed the demise of the 49ers' title hopes.

Chicago scored almost immediately. With a minute remaining in the game, the Bears came back and won the game on a George Blanda 48-yard field goal. Final score: Chicago 20, San Francisco 17.

To his credit, Buck Shaw refused to criticize Albert's gamble to the media, saying only that, "Frank has won a lot of games with this same kind of daring. He has gambled before and won. That's all I have to say."

This incident put an unbearable strain on the coach and on the team, and there is little doubt in my mind that it had a great deal to do with Frankie's decision to retire at the end of the 1952 season.

The team's publicity director, Dan McGuire, referred to Albert's decision as "Frankie's Folly on Fourth Down." It was the final straw that capped a frustrating season for Albert. It started off right from the get-go when he was told (for the first time in his entire career) that he would be a part-time quarterback. Sitting on the bench watching me play must have irked him considerably. It ended with losing four of our last six games and finishing third in the Western Division.

Frankie had been the team's undisputed leader for six years in a row, and I don't think he expected his career to end on a sour note. He was a man of great pride—a pride that had been damaged first by a quarterback controversy and second by the criticism of the fans and media alike after our defeat by the Bears.

Albert played by instinct alone, and to hell with the playbook! One time we were playing another team and leading by something like 34–0. Coach Shaw sent me in for Frankie late in the game. As I passed Albert on the way to the huddle, I asked him, "What defense are these guys in?"

"How the hell should I know?" he replied.

I honestly believe that he didn't know—either that or he didn't care. It didn't make any difference anyway; 34 points had been scored while he was at the helm.

When the defense started pressuring Frankie, he would run a draw play. It didn't matter what the defensive setup was; if they put the pressure on, he called the draw. Frankie never took plays from frequency lists or from the sideline. Everything he needed to call a game was in his head.

No one ever questioned Frankie's play-calling. His timing was flawless. When he ran a trap, it was a good time to run a trap— maybe third down and seven. It might be a passing situation and bang, he would trap the middle man, and away the guy would go.

First down was the same as fourth down to Albert. He would call a run, a pass, or a pitchout any time and any place on the field. His tactics impressed me, as did his flair for the unexpected.

I was not the signal-caller that he was, nor could I run a ballgame the way he did. But passing had always been my strength, and I have often wondered how much better a quarterback I might have been if I had been as loose and as daring as Frankie.

Throughout my professional career I have been asked if Frankie Albert—with his unique approach to quarterbacking— could play in today's game. I believe that he could, but it would have to be his way. To my way of thinking, a professional quarterback's greatness is based on winning.

Obviously, this topic is open to discussion, but outside of Otto Graham, who was perhaps the greatest of them all, Frankie was tops. He was truly a winner.

18

The Big Three:
Shaw, Strader, and Albert

BY THE TIME THE 1953 SEASON ROLLED AROUND, Frankie Albert had left the NFL and began throwing for a Canadian team and I had become the No. 1 quarterback for the 49ers.

On the first day of training camp, Coach Shaw handed me the football and said, "It's all yours, Y.A."

It may have been all mine, but the spirit of Albert was still present. A writer from the *San Francisco Chronicle* walked up to me on the practice field and asked, "How does it feel to be trying to fill Frankie's shoes?"

This was definitely a loaded question. Albert was a favorite in the Bay Area, and it was inevitable that I would be compared with him. But I did not want to say anything that would negatively reflect on him or something that would hurt the morale of our ballclub.

But on the other hand, I didn't want to give the impression that I was afraid to follow in Frankie's footsteps or that I lacked confidence in my ability as a quarterback. Either way, I knew I would probably put my foot in my mouth once more with the San Francisco press. I answered the question the best that I could. I said, "I realize it's going to be tough to replace Frankie. He was a great quarterback, but I have faith in myself, and I think I can get the job done for the 49ers."

The following day the *Chronicle* headlined the story: "Tittle Defies Ghost of Albert!"

Of course this was never said or even implied. I wasn't defying any ghosts. All I had said was that I believed I could do the job. A quarterback's attitude is contagious—it infects every man on the squad. If he is the least bit unsure of himself, this uncertainty is transmitted right down the line, and the ballclub dies.

I realized the odds that faced me as Albert's successor, but I was confident that I could gain the faith of the 49ers team. And this is exactly what I told the *Chronicle* sportswriter.

Despite my hopes, the headline stirred up a big fuss at camp. Some people construed it as a blow to Frankie. There was resentment, and I could sense it right from the start.

From that point on I promised myself that I would tell the sportswriters to go elsewhere for their stories. It was the second time my comments had been misinterpreted and blown out of proportion.

Even though I had been a starter with the Colts in 1948 and 1949, 1953 was my first year as a regular quarterback in the NFL. There was no comparison between the old AAFC and the NFL. Things were now more organized, the players were better athletes, and the crowds were much bigger.

Although Albert, Norm Standlee, Alyn Beals, and a few of the other 49ers veterans had retired, the '53 squad was not short on talent. Hugh McElhenny was in his second season and going strong, as was Joe Perry, who was still a top runner. Joe Arenas was still plugging away, Gordy Soltau was at his peak as a receiver and as a place-kicker, and Billy Wilson was becoming a fine pass-catcher. My old Texas sidekick, Bill Johnson, was a solid center.

And as rookies go, Buck Shaw kept 14 of them on the roster—one of them was defensive lineman Charlie Powell.

The 49ers were on a roll in the opener against the Philadelphia Eagles—that is, right after a 20-minute free-for-all between Charlie Powell and Philadelphia's star receiver, Bobby Walston. The fight spread like wildfire. Two of the Eagles went after McElhenny. Mac swung his helmet with one hand and threw punches with the other. Observing that his situation was perilous, several members of the 49ers band joined the battle, using clarinets as weapons.

The fight ended in a draw, but not the game. We beat the Eagles 31–21 and found new team spirit that carried us to a 9–3 record. This was the best performance in San Francisco history, but unfortunately Detroit was 10–2 that year. We had to settle for second place in the Western Division.

Observing that his situation was perilous, several members of the 49ers band joined the battle, using clarinets as weapons.

McElhenny was an amazing runner, and rarely did a game go by that he didn't perform some amazing feat.

The week after we beat Philly, the Rams had us down 30–28 with less than three minutes left in the game. The ball was on our own 20, and I knew that Los Angeles would be looking for the long desperation pass.

On first down, I glanced at Mac in the huddle and said, "They're expecting a bomb. Let's go with a screen right."

"Okay," Mac said.

I could tell he was just itching to get loose with the football.

With the L.A. secondary playing deep, it was easy to throw a short screen pass to McElhenny in the right flat. Leo Nomellini took out the nearest Rams defender with a smashing block, and Mac was off to the races. He swiveled down the sideline, eluding tacklers every step of the way. He was finally shoved out of bounds on the 9-yard line. He had run 71 yards! I called three running plays to kill the clock, and then Soltau booted a field goal that gave us a 31–30 victory.

Mac was really something in his prime. In my opinion, there never has been another open-field runner like him.

Hugh once told me that he always ran scared, but it wasn't just because of gridiron opponents—it was the memory of a boyhood incident. When he was six years old, he talked his way into a pickup game on a vacant lot in Watts (on the outskirts of Los Angeles). The owner of the property arrived minutes later with a shotgun. He pulled the trigger and several pellets lodged into Mac's backside as he fled the scene.

"When I carry the ball, I think of that old farmer and his shotgun. It makes me run faster," said Mac.

I couldn't have asked for two better backs than McElhenny and Joe Perry. They could run both inside and outside, catch the ball, and block. They contributed to making me look good for the many years we played together, and I will always appreciate what they did for the team and for me.

The Sunday following McElhenny's great run and our defeat of the Rams, I suffered the most serious injury of my professional career—up to that time. I fractured my cheekbone in three places!

We were playing the Detroit Lions when I made the decision to run a bootleg play. I started from the 5 and made it all the way to the end zone before Jack Christiansen grabbed my arm and spun me around. In the end, my face met with Jim David's knee. I could hear the bones crunching in my cheek. It was some of the worst pain I had ever experienced.

The fact that I had scored really didn't matter because we lost the game 24–21. I ended up in a Detroit hospital, where they removed 16 bone chips from my face. To hold the cheek's shape, an inflated balloon was inserted into my face. I was forced to stay in that hospital for a week and missed the Chicago game. Jimmy Powers, one of the 49ers defensive backs, took my place and quarterbacked the club to a 35–28 victory over the Bears.

That broken cheekbone in 1953 was the beginning of a string of injuries resulting from Frankie Albert's favorite play, the bootleg. The bootleg may have been beneficial to my career, but it was detrimental to my body.

I ended up in a Detroit hospital, where they removed 16 bone chips from my face.

In 1962 we were playing Detroit when I suffered a brain concussion going into the end zone on a bootleg. That same year my face was sliced open in a Pittsburgh game when I rolled out and made a run for it. In the opening game against Baltimore in 1963, I scored a touchdown on a bootleg. I was tackled so viciously that the force caused one of my lungs to partially collapse. Bootlegs against Green Bay and Dallas left me with back injuries that kept me on the injured list.

After the cheekbone incident in Detroit in '53, a special face mask was made for me. I received it just in time for our next game with the Lions. During the competition, I threw only one pass—which was unfortunately intercepted. We ended up losing to Detroit a second time, 14–10. Things looked better the following week when we beat the Rams 31–27 in front of more than 90,000 fans in the Los Angeles Coliseum. Our Southern California rival had us down 27–24 with five minutes left in the game. Fortunately, we were able to move the ball 85 yards down the field and win the game when I hit Soltau with a 17-yard touchdown pass. There were 12 seconds left in the game when Gordy fell into the end zone.

Those 1953 battles with the Rams were two of the most thrilling football games I ever played in. Los Angeles had everything—exciting touchdowns, long scoring plays, and last-minute drama. They drew tremendous crowds at both Kezar Stadium and the Coliseum. Not only did they establish professional football on the West Coast, but they fulfilled one of Tony Morabito's dreams. The other, a championship for San Francisco, had yet to be achieved.

The excitement and enthusiasm from the '53 season carried over to the following year. The 1954 49ers won seven straight preseason games and were regarded as the top team in the league.

Not only did we have McElhenny and Perry, but we had John Henry Johnson. We were nicknamed the "Million Dollar Backfield." I'm not sure how much I was worth, but the others were priceless running backs—possibly the three greatest ball carriers ever to play in the same backfield.

John Henry had come to the 49ers from Canada via a trade with Pittsburgh. He gave us the strongest offense in professional football. Perry led the NFL in rushing that year for the second straight time, and Johnson was right behind him. Mac finished in the top 10 despite missing almost half the season with a broken shoulder.

Hugh wasn't the only 49er on the 1954 injured list. Our entire ballclub was ravished with injuries. I had never seen anything like it. It was a wonder that we won at all, much less seven games.

In our opening game we beat Washington 41–7. Arnold Galiffa, our second-string quarterback, broke his hand. That was the beginning of our downfall.

The following week we tied Los Angeles 24–24 but not before I had broken my left hand and John Henry went down with multiple injuries. Before the season was even half over, we lost our two best linebackers, Hardy Brown and Don Burke. We almost lost our entire secondary in Jim Cason, Rex Berry, and John Williams. The remainder of the season saw us as a patchwork ballclub. Bill Jessup, an offensive end, wound up playing defensive halfback, as did John Henry. Buck Shaw was forced to utilize the league's most feared ball carrier on defense because he had no one else. Every week Buck had to juggle players back and forth. It was remarkable that he was even able to field an offense and defense on the same day!

The problem wasn't that the 49ers couldn't score; we finished with 313 points, and I completed 170 passes as Perry and Johnson ran wild on the field. The problem was that we couldn't stop anybody! Halfway through the schedule the Rams scored 42 points on us and Detroit slammed us 48–7. The beating we took from the Lions was Buck Shaw's worst defeat. I feel that this game marked the beginning of the end for him as the coach of the 49ers.

Owner Tony Morabito had always been fair with his players and coaches, but Tony wanted a championship in the worst way. He really believed that the 1954 team would be the one to win it for him. Even with all our injuries, Tony believed that Coach Shaw could work enough miracles to bring a championship to San Francisco. Buck was a sound coach and a top football man, but he was not a miracle worker. Our 1954 season ended with a 7–5 record, but it was too little, too late.

> *The beating we took from the Lions was Buck Shaw's worst defeat.*

After our final game with the Colts, Buck Shaw was notified that his contract as 49ers head coach would not be renewed. His dismissal kicked up quite a controversy, but when you don't win, change is inevitable. Buck's easygoing style of coaching had not produced a championship for San Francisco. On the other hand, Paul Brown's rigid, severe tactics had brought Cleveland several world titles. Perhaps the time had arrived to try it Brown's way.

Tony's reasons for firing Shaw were known only to Tony. It had been said that when the 49ers were losing money, Tony had asked Buck to take a percentage of the club in lieu of part of his salary. Coach refused, and the story has it that Morabito never really forgave him.

The 1955 San Francisco 49ers season was the team's sixth year in the NFL. It was also a nightmare. Our record was 4–8, and we placed fifth in our division. The only team who played worse than we did was Detroit; they had a 3–9 record.

Coach Shaw's successor was Red Strader, who died at the end of the year after being fired by Morabito. I had 28 passes intercepted, the second-worst showing by a quarterback in NFL history.

Strader was the opposite of Coach Shaw. He spoke very fast and was a stern disciplinarian. He had coached briefly in the All-America Conference and believed in total organization. Under his regime, he was determined to eliminate the stigma that the 49ers were "the country club of the NFL"—a name bestowed upon us by a rival owner.

Coach Strader's attitude reflected that of his assistant coaches. One of those coaches was Howard "Red" Hickey, who had been with the Rams for 14 years. He was really tough.

There was one assistant, though, who did not fit into this new coaching staff—Frankie Albert. Albert had returned from Canada to rejoin the 49ers staff. Frankie hadn't changed a bit. He was still an easygoing, relaxed guy.

But changes were in the works. Training camp was moved from Menlo Park to St. Mary's College. Making the adjustment from Buck Shaw's style to Red Strader's was not an easy task for the 49ers veterans, myself included. Red had publicly announced his intention to take "any measures that [would] make the 49ers a winning football team." Many of us wondered where, if at all, we would fit in Strader's plans.

Training camp showed us just what kind of micromanager Red Strader really was. As we came on to the practice field, we were told to jog, never to walk! The same applied when we left the field. You *always* wore your helmet and kept track of time by the clock at St. Mary's College. Everything was detailed, step-by-step, minute-by-minute.

At night he patrolled the halls of the dorm from 10:30 to 11:00—personally making sure that everyone was in his room. Although he did look quite ridiculous wearing that Ebenezer Scrooge nightshirt with matching nightcap. All that was missing was the candle and candleholder. Breakfast was at 7:30 AM, and you had better be there *exactly* at 7:30!

Strader's new-age approach was not popular with the players. After all, we had all been used to the philosophy and style of Buck Shaw. By our third week of training camp at St. Mary's, the guys began to visibly complain. Upon losing a couple of preseason games, it got worse. The guys began to talk, and the blame was passed on to several individuals. Disapproval of the coaches and administration was also a hot topic of discussion. This became an extremely serious matter for the ballclub.

However, in the end, Coach Strader was made the scapegoat for the 49ers' failures.

I must admit that I was just as much a part of Coach Strader's dismissal as the rest of the squad. We had just returned home from playing the Colts in Baltimore, where we were defeated. After the game owner Tony Morabito dropped by our dressing

I must admit that I was just as much a part of Coach Strader's dismissal as the rest of the squad.

room to say a few words. He told us that he was only going to stay for "a few minutes." That few minutes ended up being over *two hours!*

One of the players mentioned to Tony that the team couldn't win under Strader's strict regimentation. Morabito's reaction was one of surprise. Apparently he had been unaware that such resentment existed between the players and coaches.

When we lost our eighth and final ballgame of the 1955 season, the owners requested a meeting with Strader. Red was asked if the 4–8 record was a true indication of 49ers personnel. Without hesitation Red replied, "Absolutely! In fact, I'd say we were lucky to win four games this year!"

Red had sealed his own fate.

I have always regretted taking part in that clubhouse meeting with Morabito, but I could hardly have avoided it. Even though I didn't always agree with Strader's policies, I admired him as a person and respected him as a coach. He was hard on the ballplayers, but he was always behind them. He fought to get an increase in our meal money when we were on the road and got us better beds in training camp. Red was always there to fight battles for the players, but there were times when it was difficult for us to believe that he was really on our side.

Football under Buck Shaw was fun; under Red Strader it was drudgery. It became a regimented business where you clocked in every morning and kept your nose to the grindstone until Red blew the final whistle at quitting time. No one ever smiled, laughed, or clowned around; it was strictly business as usual. Buck used to throw the ball on to the field and let us run a few plays. Strader had us worrying about technique, steps, position, the reason for this, the strategy for that—it was awful.

Red's dedicated approach might have worked if we were winning, but in 1955 the 49ers were a losing team, and his methods backfired. By the end of the season, he was going in one direction while the team was going in another.

The transition from Shaw to Strader never came to be. Red died shortly after his dismal from the 49ers, and I was sorry to hear of his passing.

In 1956 Tony Morabito hired Frankie Albert as the 49ers' new head coach. Although Frankie's coaching experience was limited to a couple of spring practices at Stanford and the Naval Academy, I was happy to hear of his appointment. The team thought that they would be returning to the happy times of Buck Shaw, but it seemed that Albert the coach was a different man than Albert the happy-go-lucky quarterback.

Frankie's Jekyll-and-Hyde personality came to light on the first day of training camp. One reporter wrote the following about Albert: "When Albert got the 49er job, even his friends feared his dislike of practice routine might be his undoing. Small details were not his style. Only grand strategy appealed to him. But the sun hadn't yet sunk behind the Moraga hills after the first practice when those who had him pegged as a 'no detail' man realized they were wrong. The place reeked with organization. Frankie had mapped specific, sensible work schedules months ago, and they were followed almost to the split second. Things went off like clockwork."

Albert's first decision was to retain Strader's entire coaching staff. I always suspected that Frankie's rigid approach to coaching was inspired by Red Hickey. Under Strader, Hickey had been end coach, but Frankie had made him a backfield coach and gave him greater latitude in decision making. Red thrived on authority. Albert was aware of this and delegated more and more responsibility to Red as the season wore on. Not having a great deal of experience in coaching, Frankie appeared grateful to have a veteran coach like Hickey to lean on.

As a quarterback Albert was reckless, but as a head coach he was extremely conservative. There were many times when we had a short-yardage situation at midfield and Frankie frantically would signal from the sideline for a punt. As a player he would have run for the yard and damn the percentages.

It wasn't Frankie's conservative style that bothered me; it was his sudden and unexplainable decision to call the game from the sideline.

Paul Brown had won five straight divisional championships for Cleveland by sending in the plays to Otto Graham, but Albert was not Brown, nor I Graham. And the 49ers were definitely not the Cleveland Browns. Graham and his players had grown up under the messenger-boy signal system and were accustomed to it. They knew no other way to win games, and they did not object to Brown's sideline quarterbacking as long as it proved successful.

Play-calling from the sideline was not my idea of how to play quarterback. After playing in the league for nine years and calling my own plays, I now found myself standing in the huddle waiting for Albert to send in the plays with our two ends, Clyde Connor and Gordy Soltau. Gordy and Clyde would run into the huddle and say, "Frankie says to run a 37 Slant."

So, like a parrot, I repeated the play to the guys: "37 Slant." And that was the extent of my quarterbacking. In my opinion a pro quarterback can't call a winning game if he does no more than parrot someone else's instructions. To be effective, a quarterback needs to have the *feel* of the game, outsmart and outthink the defense in order to set them up and finish them off his own way. A quarterback must lead his ballclub through his own strength, knowledge, skill, and imagination. With Albert—or possibly Red

Hickey—sending in the plays, I was detached from the action.

I had often wondered what Frankie's reaction would have been if Buck Shaw had called the plays for him when he was quarterbacking the team. Most likely he would have quit.

Play-calling from the sideline was not my idea of how to play quarterback.

I may have been frustrated, but I was not a quitter. But then neither was I a good quarterback, because I did not have control of my team. In 1956 the 49ers continued to be a losing team and lost six of our first seven games.

A rookie from Michigan State named Earl Morrall replaced me after the fifth game, but by that time I didn't really care. Frankie insisted on sticking with the messenger system, and for the first time in my football career, my heart wasn't in the game.

I don't remember exactly how it happened, but one day I said something about not liking the plays Albert was sending in. That was a big mistake on my part, but my frustration was growing with each defeat, and I lost control.

Frankie asked me to meet him in his office at Kezar Stadium the following day. Tony Morabito was there when I arrived. For the first time I saw a different side of Frankie Albert—a tough, hard side. The smile was gone from his face, as was his easy manner. His voice was cold and firm.

"Y.A., I know you don't like me calling the plays. You said so the other day, and everybody heard you. But I'm the coach, damn it, and I'll call the plays and you'll do what I tell you. If you don't want to go along, well, maybe we'll make some changes."

I stood there stunned.

"Okay," I said. "But I still don't like it."

Morabito never said a word, but it was obvious that he was the authority figure behind Frankie's firm stand. His presence at the meeting made me aware that he stood behind his coach. Even in all my frustration, I admired Tony for his loyalty to Albert.

I sat out the next two games while Morrall did the quarter-backing and Albert did the signal-calling. We ended up losing both games. Detroit beat us 17–13, and the Rams trounced us 30–6. We were in last place.

The Tuesday following our loss to the Rams, Frankie conceded that maybe he had been wrong about trying to call the game from the bench. He pulled me aside in the locker room and said, "It's all yours from now on, Y.A."

Albert may have been stubborn, but he was smart enough to see that his plan wasn't working.

What I think happened is that Frankie overlooked one vital fact when he decided to send in plays. He had been a great quarter-back, but his greatness was based on his ability to *improvise* and unite the team with one electrifying pass or run. This is what made him a winner on the field, but from the bench he was unable to instill that same emotion to the team as he had from the huddle.

With control now back in my hands, we defeated Green Bay 17–16, tied the Eagles, and then played out the season with wins over Baltimore at Baltimore and Green Bay and Baltimore at home.

I would like to make it clear that I alone was not responsible for this sudden about-face at the end of the 1956 campaign. It just seemed that the players responded better to a play called in the huddle than to one carried in from the bench. The team was loose and relaxed and got the *feel* of the game, and the result was that we began to win.

The 49ers finished third behind Chicago and Detroit, respectively, with a 5–6–1 record. Frankie gained experience and wisdom, and we all got ready for the big title push in 1957.

19

1957: The Year of the Alley-Oop

THE 1957 SEASON WAS THE YEAR OF THE ALLEY-OOP PASS. It was also the year that the 49ers were defeated by the Detroit Lions for the National Football League's Western Division title.

Losing the division title was tough, but the death of our beloved owner, Tony Morabito, was devastating.

Several years prior, Tony had suffered a heart attack and was cautioned by his doctors to remove himself from the pressures of professional football. But the game was his life, and his dream was to see his team win a championship.

Disregarding the advice of his doctors, Tony continued to run the franchise, worked day and night, and traveled with the team on road trips.

On October 25 the 49ers played the Chicago Bears at Kezar Stadium. During the first half of the game Tony suffered a massive heart attack. In a moment of excitement, he slumped over in his box and was dead before he could be rushed to the hospital. We were trailing the Bears 17–7 in the third period when Dr. Bill O'Grady came in to the locker room and told us the sad news.

Needless to say, we were all in shock. Not only was Tony our boss, but he was also our friend. Morabito had remained the one constant throughout the series of coaching changes and player

In a moment of excitement, Tony slumped over in his box and was dead before he could be rushed to the hospital.

shake-ups. Upon hearing the news, I remember how Leo Nomellini and Joe Perry cried. I struggled to fight back the tears.

As we took the field, we took our grief out on the Bears. Nomellini, tears streaming down his face, savagely rushed Bears quarterback Ed Brown, forcing him to throw the ball. Bill Kerchman, our big tackle, intercepted and ran 54 yards for a touchdown. Our defense continued to pressure Brown, and in the fourth quarter Dicky Moegle intercepted another Chicago pass. Moegle ran all the way to the Bears' 19-yard line. Joe Perry charged his way to the 11, and then I hit Billy Wilson for the winning touchdown.

As we took the field, we took our grief out on the Bears.

With 12 minutes left to play in the game, Chicago had the ball for 25 plays, but the devastating 49ers defense swarmed all over Brown and running back Willie Galimore. The game ended when Moegle intercepted another pass to clinch the win for San Francisco, 21–17.

We never gave Tony his championship, but we sure rolled over the Bears that bleak day in Kezar Stadium.

The 49ers of 1957 were really a great team. Our record of 8–4 was good enough to tie Detroit for the Western Division championship. Every game was a nail-biter. In six of our eight wins, the victory margin was seven or less points. We beat the Rams 23–20, Chicago 21–17, the Bears again by the same score (the day Tony died), Detroit 35–31, Baltimore 17–13, and Green Bay 27–20. Most of these victories were accomplished on electrifying fourth-quarter comebacks.

Ironically, Detroit beat us in the same fashion when they came back from a 27–7 fourth-quarter deficit to whip us 31–17 and clinch the Western Division title.

For me the death of Tony and the loss of the divisional title were devastating, but that '57 season was the most rewarding of my career. I completed 63 percent of my passes—a personal best—and was named the NFL Player of the Year.

The 49ers gave the appearance of being a mediocre ballclub, but looks can be deceiving. We proved that as we pulled out wins one after the other and then suddenly found ourselves with a shot at the championship.

In retrospect, many of those comeback victories were made possible by a wide receiver from the College of Idaho by the name of R.C. Owens. R.C. had become one of my favorite receivers and soon the Alley-Oop pass would be born.

The Alley-Oop pass was created completely by accident while practicing for a game against the Los Angeles Rams.

We had been upset in the opener by the Chicago Cardinals, 20–10. With team morale in the bucket, a win over the highly rated Rams seemed unrealistic. How could we hope to beat L.A. when we couldn't even control a weak team like the Cardinals?

Nearing the end of the practice session, we devoted the remainder of our time to a dummy pass scrimmage, which didn't go well to say the least. Our ends were consistently dropping balls, and our defensive linemen were rushing through before I could pick out my receivers. It was a mess.

Disgusted with it all, I decided to just throw the ball straight up into the air with no receiver in mind. At first it soared into the atmosphere, then hung there a moment, and finally floated down toward R.C. Owens, who was surrounded by three defensive backs. Just then R.C. leaped into the air and grabbed the ball while the defensive players stood there dumbfounded.

No one was more surprised than I when Owens caught that pass. Just then someone on the sideline yelled out, "Hey, that's our Alley-Oop play!"

The name caught on and so did the play. For the remainder of the week Owens and I worked on the Alley-Oop pass after regular practice had ended.

The mechanics of the play were not fancy. The concept was simple. I was to throw the ball as high and as far as I could. R.C. would jog down the field, wait for the ball to get about 14 feet from the ground, and then outjump everybody around him. This former College of Idaho basketball star could really soar through the air. At the height of his jump, he was usually head and shoulders above the defensive backs.

In the beginning, no one really took the Alley-Oop seriously. Because we all had so much fun with the maneuver, the coaches saw it more as a remedy for the team's low morale rather than a formidable weapon. But either way, R.C. and I had a lot of fun with it.

The media, on the other hand, had a field day with the new tactic, and by the time we kicked off to the Rams at Kezar that following Sunday, everyone was anticipating when the Alley-Oop would occur…everyone, that is, except the Rams, who obviously thought it was just a gimmick.

By the end of the game, Los Angeles no longer thought of the new play as a publicity stunt. After throwing two Alley-Oop passes to Owens that day, we beat the Rams by a final score of 23–20.

The first pass was thrown near the end of the first half. The 49ers held a 9–7 edge over the Rams but were hoping to score again before the half was over. With the ball on the Los Angeles 46 and 50 seconds on the clock, I dropped back and aimed the ball at the corner—throwing it as high as I could. The Rams' Don

Burroughs was covering R.C. as they both went up for the ball. Owens jumped a little higher than Burroughs and yanked the ball right out of Don's hands for the score. All of a sudden the San Francisco fans began shouting in unison, "Alley-Oop, Alley-Oop, Alley-Oop!"

In the second half of the game, the Rams came back and went ahead of us, 20–16. With less than three minutes remaining in the game, the 49ers gained possession of the ball and a last shot to score. McElhenny and J.D. Smith took it down to the Rams 11. On second down, I stepped in to the huddle and said, "We'll go for the Alley-Oop!"

That was the first time (in the huddle) I ever called the play by name, and everyone knew what to do, especially Owens.

R.C. jogged into the end zone and stood next to the Rams' defensive back, Jesse Castete. I dropped back, waited for a count or two, then heaved the ball almost straight up in the air. No one was moving! They were all just standing there looking at the ball! Even R.C. didn't seem concerned, but at just the right moment he sprang up like a cat and came down with the football hugged close to his chest. Castete didn't have a chance.

With the Alley-Oop now considered to be a legitimate weapon, the only defense against it was a defensive back who could out-leap R.C.—and at that time, no such animal existed in the NFL.

R.C. Owens was a great all-around receiver. He could catch the ball high, low, and in between. He had incredible speed for a 6'3", 200 pounder and big hands that could squeeze the football like an orange.

The week following our defeat of the Rams, Owens made an unbelievable catch against the Chicago Bears. With four minutes left in the game, Chicago was ahead 17–14. The Bears had possession of the ball and were burning the clock, but Ed Henke and Charlie Powell played great defense and forced Ed Brown to punt. Joe Arenas ran the kickoff all the way back to the San Francisco 43-yard line before fighting his way out of bounds and stopping the clock.

The following play was a screen to McElhenny for 26 yards. Next, I threw to Clyde Connor for 12, then passed to Billy Wilson for another 12. This put us on the Chicago 7.

As the ball was snapped, a Bears linebacker knocked R.C. down on the line of scrimmage. He crawled into the end zone on his hands and knees and was in position when I threw the ball toward the corner of the end zone. Owens lunged and caught the ball for the winning touchdown, ending the game with a 21–17 victory over Chicago.

A week later we were playing the Packers when an official said to me, "Hey, Y.A., when are you going to throw one of those Alley-Oop passes? I've never seen the thing."

"How about the next play?" I said.

"Great, Y.A."

I threw the ball up in the air as R.C. ran down the field and waited for the ball. As he jumped up, he batted it out of the reach of the two Green Bay players who were covering him, caught it on the rebound, and fell over the goal line for a touchdown.

The official who had requested the play walked over to me and said, "Thanks, Tittle, but don't try it again. The next time you'll be bringing down rain, and we've got a nice dry field here."

When I threw the Alley-Oop to R.C. we had been ahead of the Packers by only three points. His touchdown catch gave us a solid 24–14 victory.

Most of Owens' catches in 1957 were big, but none were more important or as spectacular as the one he made against the Detroit Lions. It was the greatest catch I had ever seen in football.

138

With 1:20 left to play in the game, the Lions were winning by a score of 31–28, and the 49ers fans began heading out of Kezar Stadium. San Francisco had received more than their share of miracles, but with time against us, pulling out a win would take more than an epiphany.

With only a minute remaining in the game, Joe Arenas ran the Lions' kickoff out to our 18-yard line. Our only hope was to throw a lot of short passes and get the ball out of bounds in order to stop the clock. We knew it was our only hope, and so did the Lions. I hit Gene Babb for one yard, and Billy Wilson caught one for 12 yards before going out of bounds. I lobbed a screen pass to McElhenny for 10 yards as he made his way to the sideline.

Mac took another screen, rushed for eight yards, and went out of bounds. He ran the ball a third time and fought his way out of bounds to the Detroit 41. By this time the fans had ceased moving toward the exits and stood in the aisles. The Alley-Oop play was all we had left, and it would be the last play of the game.

The Lions used a four-man rush, dropping everyone else into the secondary, but they still broke through my blockers. Fearing for my life, I ran back to the 50 and toward the sideline. Those massive linemen were breathing down my neck

> *By this time the fans had ceased moving toward the exits and stood in the aisles.*

every step of the way. For a moment I didn't think I would ever get the ball away. R.C. was running down the right sideline covered by the Lions' great defensive back, Jim David. They were shoulder-to-shoulder. Finally I couldn't wait any longer and let the ball fly. I threw the ball higher and farther than I ever had before. As the ball soared in the air, I was knocked down and ended up watching the remainder of the play on my backside.

Owens had made it to the 1-yard line and was standing there waiting for the ball—but he wasn't alone. Detroit's Jim David, Jack Christiansen, and Carl Karilivacz had surrounded R.C.

Owens sprang into the air, as did the Lions, but R.C. out-jumped Detroit's defense and managed to catch the ball. He fell into the end zone and we won the game 34–31.

The 1957 Western Division Playoff Game had us matched up against Detroit once more. With an Alley-Oop play early in the game, the 49ers got off to a fast 7–0 lead. Soon after, I hit McElhenny for a 47-yard touchdown and another to Gordy Soltau for a 21–0 lead. Before the half was over, Soltau added a field goal to the mix, and we walked off the field leading 24–7.

It looked like the 49ers were finally going to get a chance at the "big one," but fate had other plans for San Francisco.

Early in the third quarter Mac ran all the way to the Detroit 9, but we were stopped cold by the Lions and had to settle for another field goal by Soltau. This great defensive stand instilled Detroit with new hope and left the 49ers bewildered. Tobin Rote came in for Bobby Layne and was on fire and couldn't miss. As for San Francisco, we completely fell apart. In the end, Detroit triumphed, beating us 31–27.

20

A Changing of the Guard

IN 1959 WE PLAYED THE RAMS IN LOS ANGELES in front of 95,000 screaming fans and got crushed 56–7. It was the beginning of the end for coach Frankie Albert.

We had a 3–3 record going in to the Coliseum that day, and Frankie still believed we had a shot at the Western Division championship. The Rams thought otherwise, scoring early and often.

The following week we played Detroit and were once again beaten, 35–21. After that game Albert began to show signs of emotional stress. He approached Tony's brother, Vic Morabito—who had taken over for Tony—and told him that he intended to resign his coaching position.

"I just can't take it anymore," Frankie said. "I don't mind what they say about me, but my family has taken a lot of abuse lately, and it's not worth it. There's no other way. I'm through as soon as the season ends." Vic tried to calm him down, but Albert had made up his mind.

In reality Frankie had been under pressure right from the start of the 1958 season. After I had played a poor preseason, Frankie benched me and put in John Brodie as the No. 1 quarterback. This caused quite a protest in San Francisco. The media took sides just as they had in the Tittle/Albert controversy of 1952. One article stated, "Tittle may not have been effective in the exhibition games, but he's had slumps before and always managed to snap out of them when the chips were down."

The opposition countered with, "Tittle hasn't won it for the 49ers. Now Brodie deserves a chance."

In retrospect it was ironic for Albert to find himself in the same situation that he and I had experienced back in '51. Back then coach Buck Shaw had been pressured to bench Frankie and make room for me. Now, six years later, the circumstances had been duplicated—only this time Albert had to choose between Brodie and me.

Frankie had been criticized by a few members of the media for going with Brodie, but I have always felt that it was Hickey who made the call to bench me. He had a tremendous influence on Albert.

Red Hickey was a real football man. I seldom saw eye-to-eye with him, but I never questioned his dedication or sincerity.

Red never cared whether his players liked him or not. He never considered football to be a personality contest. The day he took over as Frankie's successor in 1959 he only had one thing to say: "All I ask is that my players give me a hundred percent on the field."

> *Red never cared whether his players liked him or not.*

When I had heard that Red had been named head coach, I felt that my days as a San Francisco 49er were numbered. Hickey was not my greatest fan, and I sensed that Brodie would soon become the team's No. 1 quarterback—a move that had originated the year before under Albert.

At the end of the 1957 season I was named the NFL's Player of the Year, but Red had Brodie start the opening game of the season in 1958. I never understood that. I at least deserved a chance to keep my starting job until Brodie proved he was better than me, but Hickey didn't operate that way. There wasn't a player alive who wasn't indispensable to Red.

At the beginning of the 1959 campaign, oddly enough, Red decided to go with me through the first seven games. We won six out of seven, and Hickey, whether he liked it or not, was at least smart enough to go with a winner.

With the season half over, the 49ers had a 6–1 record and led the Western Division by a game. Despite the success of the team, I was not having a great season by any means.

I had completed less than 46 percent of my passes and was bothered by occasional dizzy spells. Doctors had discovered that I had Meniere's disease—a rare disturbance of the middle ear, which greatly affected my balance.

These dizzy spells usually occurred during the middle of the week, but luckily by Sunday they had subsided. Still, my passing game was off—missing guys in the open by either underthrowing or overthrowing them.

Hickey requested that Dr. Bill O'Grady put me through a series of tests, but the results were inconclusive, and I was given a clean bill of health. But the spells continued, and my passing continued to decline.

The turning point for the 1959 49ers team occurred on November 15 at Wrigley Field in Chicago. We lost to the Bears 14–3, and it was here that Hickey made the decision to bench me and make Brodie his No. 1 quarterback.

Chicago scored first after taking the opening kickoff. On our first series, McElhenny ran into the clear for a pass, beating the Bears' defensive back by three yards, and I threw a ball 20 feet over his head. On the next play Billy Wilson got free, and this time I threw the ball right into the hands of a Chicago player for an interception.

I walked back to the bench shaking my head. In all my years, I had never missed two receivers the way I had just missed Mac and Billy. As I reached the sideline, Hickey gave me a disgusted look.

When the Bears punted to us a few minutes later, I started back on to the field when I heard Hickey's voice calling me back. He said, "Stay where you are, Y.A., Brodie is going in."

As Brodie ran on to the field to lead the team, I sat there on the bench. Red decided to send me back in with only five minutes to play, but after several completions I had another pass intercepted by Chicago's middle linebacker, Bill George. Again Brodie was called to replace me.

They carried me off on a stretcher, and the doctors told me that I was through for the season.

The following Sunday we played Baltimore and got bombed 48–14. The Colts hit me from three sides on a pass play, and down I went. My inner ear was fine, but the ligaments in my right knee were severely damaged. They carried me off on a stretcher, and the doctors told me that I was through for the season.

Now the way was cleared for Brodie.

21

The Beginning of the End

IN NOVEMBER 1960 THE 49ERS WERE A TEAM THAT WAS GOING nowhere, and my career as an NFL quarterback seemed to be headed in the same direction.

San Francisco had lost four of its first eight games and trailed the Packers by three games in the Western Division race. My own personal situation was much the same and just as depressing. I was 34 years old, suffering from a groin injury that had failed to respond to treatment, and collecting splinters from riding the bench behind former Stanford great John Brodie.

When Red took over in 1959, I began to lose faith in my ability. I could no longer use my skill, knowledge, or intelligence in play-calling because Red was now drawing up the game plans. The 1960 campaign would be no different.

Each week John and I never knew who would be the starter of the game. It was an uncomfortable feeling, and I believe Brodie felt as uneasy as I did. This tension began to infiltrate everything we did. The day we played the Packers in Green Bay, Brodie and I were warming up in a pass drill. Even though we didn't always know where he was, we knew that Hickey was watching us intently.

John started the game against Green Bay, but when he threw for 0–13 in the first few minutes, Hickey took him out and sent me in. Even though I had a decent second half, we still lost 41–14.

Upon returning to the West Coast, we played the Bears at Kezar. In the first period I was hit from the side, and as I fell I heard my groin muscle pop. I knew right away I was in trouble. As I was taken off the field I watched Brodie jog into the huddle.

On November 22 we held practice at Georgetown University before our game with the Baltimore Colts. It was also the day we first heard about a new offensive formation called "the shotgun."

Before practice began, Hickey gathered the team around him and passed out a new offensive scheme. "Gentlemen, we have worked out a new offensive pattern that will allow us to be victorious over Baltimore!"

We all looked at each other with doubt. Could Hickey be cracking under the stress of losing too many games? More than halfway through the season was a hell of a time to change our offense. We had enough trouble learning the old one!

More than halfway through the season was a hell of a time to change our offense.

Red knew that the shotgun would be a tough sell, so he went right to work on the team. For over four months he had drilled the ballclub in the intricacies and timing of the standard T formation. Now, with only five games left on the schedule, the familiar T was to be replaced by something called the shotgun. I have to admit that many of the players thought Red had finally lost it.

But Hickey was serious and drew some hastily sketched diagrams on paper to show us what the formation looked like. Brodie and I took our first look at the shotgun. Hickey's new offense had the quarterback standing five to seven yards behind the center, with the left end spread 10 to 15 yards from the left tackle and the right end spread three to five yards from the right tackle. The left halfback and the fullback, the two tight or running backs, were one yard outside of and a yard behind the left and right tackles, respectively. The right halfback was split far to the right, about 10 yards wider than the end on that side.

Not only did this new formation allow us to get a lot of receivers downfield, but it also allowed us to run with the ball, too.

It was obvious that Hickey had given his creation considerable thought, but the Colts were a 16-point favorite, were the defending champions, and—with Big Daddy Lipscomb, Gino Marchetti, and Art Donovan on the line—had the best defense in the league. Baltimore was well accustomed to their 4-3 defense, but Red believed we could use the shotgun and spread them out and move the ball on them before they could adjust. He was right. Brodie and the rest of the 49ers beat the Colts 30–22 for one of the biggest upsets of the season.

By the time we returned to California to play our archrivals, the Rams, the shotgun formation was the talk of the football world. The media called it a revolutionary form of attack. The offensive procedure was not really new, but Hickey's version apparently caught everyone's attention, and it was an overnight sensation.

When we met the Rams at the Coliseum the following Sunday, I was still riding the bench. The Rams were ready for the passes John threw from the spread, but they were not prepared for a strong running attack. Fullback C.R. Roberts and halfback J.D. Smith ran wild on reverses and counterplays. We had won our second straight game with the shotgun, 23–7.

The shotgun worked well in the beginning because the other teams were so set in their 4-3 defenses that they had trouble making the necessary adjustments. The shotgun forced them to change their ideas and their 4-3 thinking.

But even the new formation wasn't enough to carry San Francisco to the top in 1960. Green Bay shut us out 13–0 in the rain and mud a week later. This game uncovered one of the flaws of the shotgun. Many of our running plays were wide sweeps and reverses, but on the wet, slippery field, it was almost impossible for our backs to keep their footing when they ran laterally. The Packers, with Jim Taylor and Paul Hornung ramming straight ahead on dive plays through the middle, adapted to the poor footing more easily.

Despite this loss and our 7–5 finish that season, however, the shotgun had instilled new hope for San Francisco's future. Unfortunately it did nothing for my future with the 49ers.

22
I'll Quit Before I Play in New York!

THE SPRING OF 1961 WAS A TIME OF INDECISION and uncertainty for me. The 49ers and Hickey made it official that they were going to go with the new offense, which in turn created rumors that I would be traded.

The 49ers took the first step when they drafted an All-American tailback out of UCLA named Billy Kilmer. Billy could scramble as well as throw the option pass, which made him a perfect candidate for the shotgun formation. Kilmer was also the kind of player who could complement John Brodie as the deep man in the formation.

There were times when I said to myself, "The hell with it. Quit this damned game. You have been at it too long anyway." But a moment later I'd tell myself, "Come back for another year and show them you're still a good quarterback. Don't let them shotgun you out of football!"

Losing sleep and fighting this insidious battle with myself, I decided to get away from it all for a while—from the city, the media, and the rumors. Minnette and I packed up the kids and drove to Las Vegas for a short vacation.

My second day in Vegas, I was playing golf when I ran into Elroy Hirsch. Crazylegs was a terrific end for the Rams and was now the general manager of the Los Angeles ballclub. I had known and admired him for many years.

Elroy asked me what I was doing in Vegas. I told him I needed a break from the 49ers and the media.

"I'm glad you brought that up," Hirsch said. "Would you be interested in playing for the Rams?"

He caught me completely by surprise. The thought of playing for Los Angeles never entered my mind, but all of a sudden it sounded pretty good. I told Elroy that I would definitely be interested. I even went so far as to tell him, "I'll never play in New York or anywhere else. I'll quit if they send me back east!"

> *The thought of playing for Los Angeles never entered my mind, but all of a sudden it sounded pretty good.*

My insurance business was in Palo Alto, California, and was prospering. I felt it would be unfair to leave my partner, Milton Iverson, alone to run the company by himself. It also didn't appeal to me to have to leave Minnette, the kids, and our home in Atherton, California.

I wanted to be fair with Elroy and told him that I still wanted to play for the 49ers, but if they were going to trade me, then I would want to play for the Rams.

"Fair enough," he said. "You will be hearing from me."

Back home in Atherton I waited for something to break, but the weeks continued to pass and nothing was happening. I had finally had enough and decided to confront both Hickey and Morabito. I called the 49ers office and made an appointment for the following morning.

When I arrived at the facility, Vic Morabito was already in Hickey's office. I came right to the point and asked, "Where do I stand with your football team?"

"I'm going to be honest with you, Y.A." he said. "We might make a trade for you if we can work things out with Los Angeles. They seem to be interested in you."

"That's good, because I will retire if you try to trade me back east," I said.

Then I asked him, "What if you can't make a deal with the Rams?"

Without hesitation, Hickey made it clear that they were going with the shotgun and if I wanted to play football, I would have to come to training camp and take my chances.

I then knew where I stood with the organization.

"We will let you know if anything develops with the Los Angeles trade," he said.

I left the 49ers office feeling alone and unwanted. This had been my ballclub, and now it no longer wanted me or needed me. It hurt.

I decided to shake off the depression and was determined I would play football again. I had spent too many years in competition to throw in the towel—especially now. I made up my mind to get into the best shape I could.

Months passed, and there was still no word about a trade. I reported to training camp at St. Mary's College in July. I was really ready to play football. I weighed in at 194 pounds, my legs were in good condition, and my arm had never felt stronger. I could throw the ball as well as Brodie and better than Kilmer.

When we traveled to Portland, Oregon, to play the New York Giants, Hickey named Brodie and me as the quarterbacks. The pregame strategy against the Giants was to have Brodie open the game and run the shotgun; I would play the second half and run the standard T formation.

The Giants led 14–13 at the half, but Hickey decided to keep Brodie in for one more quarter. After New York added another touchdown for a 21–13 lead, Red waved me off the bench and sent me in at the start of the final period. I had just 15 minutes to play my hand.

With the ball on the San Francisco 34-yard line, I sent Bernie Casey up the middle on a trap for six yards. Next J.W. Lockett went around the right end for nine yards. Then I completed a 15-yarder to Lockett. We were on our way. From the Giants' 31-yard line, Lockett swept the right end for a touchdown. Tommy Davis converted, and we trailed by one point, 21–20.

Late in the period I was moving the club down the field when one of my passes, intended for Monty Stickles, was intercepted by Erich Barnes and our scoring threat ended. All in all I had a good fourth quarter against New York.

The media had mixed emotions about my performance. One said that I had played well and that Hickey wouldn't dare trade me. The other stated that I had played too well and by staying would put pressure on Brodie and create an uneasy situation for Hickey and Morabito.

Unintentionally I had backed Hickey into a corner, and soon I received the word that Hickey wanted to see me in his office.

One look at Red's face as I walked into the room was enough to tell me it was all over.

One look at Red's face as I walked into the room was enough to tell me it was all over.

"Well, Y.A.," he said, "it has finally happened. We have traded you to the New York Giants for Lou Cordileone."

I immediately asked myself, *Who the hell is Lou Cordileone? They didn't even bother to trade a name ballplayer for me!*

Red continued, "I have talked to the Giants. They need you, and they are very happy to get you. I want you to understand that. They have Charlie Conerly but don't feel they can get a whole season out of him at his age.

"I'll admit you have been throwing the ball better than anyone in camp, but we need a guard desperately, so we traded for Cordileone."

Tittle for a guard named Cordileone? Boy, that took me down a peg!

I returned to my room to pack my bags for the last time. It was tough holding back the tears.

As I walked across the practice field, I was immediately aware of the buzz that was sweeping through the players. I was in civvies, and they all knew what that meant. You would never see a ballplayer in street clothes at practice unless he was hurt or on his way out. And I wasn't hurt.

Hickey blew his whistle and ordered everyone up. I looked around at the players and began searching for the right words to say. Finally I got going. "Fellows, I guess you all know by now that I have just been traded to the New York Giants. This is part of being a professional athlete. I don't like it any more than you would, but I accept it. I hope none of you will feel sorry for me. I don't need sympathy." It was so quiet that my words seemed to echo in the breeze.

I continued, "I have gotten everything a man can get from football. San Francisco has been good to me. I owe everything to the 49ers and the Morabitos. I don't want any of you, despite your personal feelings, to hold this thing against Red Hickey or his staff. They have only done what they think is best for the 49ers. Maybe if the situation were reversed, I would make the same move Red made today. That's all I have to say except good-bye, good luck, and thanks."

As I ended my talk, I began to choke up. I looked around the circle of players and noticed that R.C. Owens and J.D. Smith were crying. It really broke me up inside.

153

I shook hands with most of the players and said good-bye. It was all over; I was an ex-49er.

Just down the road from St. Mary's I stopped at a roadside phone and called Minnette. I wanted to break the news to her before she heard it from the media. When I told her I had been traded, there was nothing but silence on the other end of the phone. Then I heard her say, "Well, Y.A., what now?"

"I don't know...I really don't. We'll talk about it when I get home."

The drive home gave me a chance to think as a thousand thoughts raced through my mind. I looked at both the pros and the cons of the situation, but as I neared home I still had not made up my mind whether to quit or to play for New York—something I swore I would never do.

The thought of leaving the West Coast bothered me, but then again I was not entirely certain that I was ready to step down either.

As I pulled up to my house, a group of men surrounded the area. I immediately knew that they were from the media. As I shouldered my way toward the door, they closed in on me. I promised I would let them know my decision as soon as possible. They informed me that they were on a deadline and would wait outside until they heard from me.

As I pulled up to my house, a group of men surrounded the area.

When I got inside the house my in-laws were there, the phone was ringing off the hook, and finally Minnette let a few of the reporters into the living room.

My wife and I went into another room and closed the door. She could see that I was unsure as to what we should do. Together we looked at the positive and negative aspects of our situation. Still without any decision, my mother-in-law came into the room and

154

said, "Well, if you two are worrying about the children, don't. I will be glad to stay here and take care of them. It will give me a chance to spoil them a bit. Minnette can join you in New York in a month or so, and then we will send the youngsters back for a week at Thanksgiving."

Grandma made it sound pretty good. Minnette and I both agreed to the trade.

I walked into the living room and told the writers and photographers that I had decided to report to the Giants. As soon as the media had gone, I slumped down on the sofa completely exhausted.

Just then the phone rang. It was Allie Sherman calling from Oregon. After exchanging greetings, I told him what was on my mind.

"Am I just an insurance quarterback in your plans, or do I get a chance to play?"

His answer was right to the point. "You'll get all the football you want with the Giants. Conerly is my quarterback right now, but I have an open mind. Besides, we have some concerns about Charlie going all the way at his age. I didn't trade for you so you could sit on the bench. We want to win this thing, and we think you can do it for us—you and Charlie."

Now everything was clear.

The phone rang again, and this time it was Frank Gifford calling from his home in Bakersfield, California. Giff was an All-Pro halfback with the Giants for many years and had retired after the 1960 season. He was doing some TV and commercial work on the West Coast. We had been friends for many years, and it was good to hear his voice.

Little did I know that Frank would make a comeback in pro football the following year and that he and I would have roles in two straight Eastern Division championships for the Giants.

Gifford told me the same things that Sherman had said earlier.

"Charlie Conerly is my closest friend, Y.A., but I don't believe he can do it by himself this year. The Giants definitely need another experienced quarterback. They need you!"

The day before I would not have gone to New York for all the money in the world, but now I could hardly wait!

Third Quarter

The New York Giants, 1961 to 1964

23

The New Kid in Camp

THE FOLLOWING MORNING I FLEW INTO SALEM, OREGON, to begin training camp at Willamette University with Allie Sherman and his New York Giants.

The day was warm and lazy, and I was awed by the beauty of the campus. But I was not there to admire the scenery; I was there to play football.

It was lunchtime, so I knew the club would be in the dining hall. As I made my way to the steps, I suddenly I felt uncomfortable and experienced an uneasy feeling in the pit of my stomach—like a kid going to school for the first time. Even though I knew I was a Giant, I sure didn't feel like one at that moment; I felt more like a visitor.

When a new guy came to the 49ers, everybody made him feel comfortable and welcomed. With the Giants it was another story. The defensive guys like Sam Huff and Andy Robustelli were a unit all their own. They didn't care for the offense—or anyone else for that matter—one way or the other. They hadn't had a new face in their group for four years. The word around the NFL was that a rookie would just be wasting his time if he were trying to make the Giants' defensive team.

On the offense there was Charlie Conerly, Pat Summerall, Kyle Rote, and Alex Webster. They had been playing together for at least 10 or 12 years. It wasn't likely that they would welcome a newcomer like me.

All of a sudden I heard someone say, "Hey, are you going to stand out there all day, or do you want to have some lunch?"

Allie Sherman was standing in the doorway, and the sound of his voice brought me back to reality.

My first meal with the Giants was far from a memorable event. I first sat down with Sherman. We talked some football, and then he turned me over to Don Heinrich, who was the backfield coach. We talked more football. I suspected they were feeling me out, and I was anxious to know what they thought of me.

Billy Stits, who played briefly for the 49ers, came over and said hello after lunch, but there was not much response from the other Giants players.

It is customary in most professional football training camps for the ballplayers to go into town and hoist a couple of beers before dinner. That was also true of the Giants. Each day I waited in my room for them to come by and get me, but it didn't happen. My acceptance by the Giants would not come easy.

The most difficult phase of my adjusting from San Francisco to New York was in learning the play calls. They were the complete opposite of everything that I had learned and known with San Francisco, but then everything in New York seemed backward.

Our first game was against the Rams, and on the day we flew to Los Angeles, Allie asked me to sit next to Don Heinrich on the plane. He told me that Don would help me with the plays.

The following night, Saturday, August 19, we played the Rams at the Coliseum—my first game as a Giant.

At the start of the fourth quarter the Giants were leading 17–3 when Sherman looked down the bench and motioned me to come over to the sideline.

"You ready to go in?" he asked.

"I don't know any plays, Al, but I'm ready to play if you want me to."

"You know the 37 Slant, don't you?" he inquired.

"Sort of," I answered.

"Well, go in and call a 37 Slant, then, just to get the feel of things."

With that, he slapped me on the rear end and I was on my way out to the center of the field.

The ball was on the Giants' 46-yard line when I stuck my head into the huddle for the first time and said, "37 Slant on three."

Ray Wietecha snapped the ball on three, but I never got a handle on it. I was all thumbs. I bobbled the exchange and then dropped the ball. When I scooped it up and started to run, I saw two big Rams bearing down on me. Now, I never had been famous for my broken-field running, and I did not intend to establish a reputation at that particular moment, not with those big tackles heading my way. The only thing I could do was fall to the ground and hold the ball close to my chest. As I hit the turf, both Rams hit me with their knees square in the back, breaking the transverse processes.

I felt a jagged pain leap up my back, and I knew right away it was something bad. I just laid there on the field with my nose pressing against the dirt. How embarrassing. One play, and I was out of the game. Here I was worrying about my leg, and now my back was injured. I was an old man by pro standards, and there I was stretched out on the Coliseum floor like I had been shot through the head.

I felt a jagged pain leap up my back, and I knew right away it was something bad.

The trainers hauled me off the field. What an exit! I was ashamed—so ashamed that I wouldn't even look in Sherman's

161

direction. In my mind I was thinking, *I bet Lou Cordileone would have looked mighty good to the Giants right now.*

That was my debut for the New York Giants. The game ended in a 17–17 tie. My back was so sore that I couldn't even sit down in the club's chartered plane. I was hurting, tired, and discouraged.

The next morning the bad news was made official. Giants team physician, Dr. Francis Sweeny, took me to Salem Hospital for X-rays. The X-rays clearly showed that two transverse processes were broken.

I shuddered when Doc Sweeny told me, "You will be out at least five weeks."

"Five weeks! Are you sure?" I asked.

"Yes, I'm sure. I have seen a lot of these injuries, and there's no way to speed the healing process. And don't forget, it takes even longer for us old fellows."

I returned to Willamette University in street clothes to watch practice and sat in the back row at the team meetings. But there was one positive development that occurred at that time—some of the Giants veterans had accepted me into their inner circle. The first two were safeties Jim Patton and his sidekick, Dick Nolan. They came by my room and asked me to go with them for a beer. Gradually the others warmed up to me, and the acceptance barrier was broken.

24

The Trade for Del Shofner

THE GIANTS' PERMANENT TRAINING CAMP WAS AT FAIRFIELD University in Connecticut. It was a beautiful school set above Long Island Sound on an old estate. It looked more like a country club than a university.

Practice resumed the next day, but without me. Sherman wouldn't even allow me to put on sweats. I felt like a spectator. It was really embarrassing!

A few days later I got word that Allie wanted to see me in his room. Reminded of St. Mary's College, when Red Hickey summoned me to his office, I thought, *The Giants aren't giving up on me already!* But I hadn't been asked to bring in my playbook. I was still a little concerned.

When I walked in to Sherman's room he motioned me to sit on the bed and then asked, "What do you think of Del Shofner?"

Shofner was the Rams' end, and obviously the Giants were interested in making a trade for him, but first Allie wanted to get the opinion of the players and coaches.

Before I could answer Allie's question, he continued. "We might get Del in a deal, but first I'm trying to find out what his trouble was in Los Angeles last year. He was great his first three years, but last season something went wrong. He caught only 12 passes for the Rams, and the year before that he had 47. It just doesn't add up."

"I spoke with him at the Pro Bowl last January, Allie," I said. "As far as I know, he dropped a couple of passes against San Francisco last year and the club lost confidence in him. Then he lost confidence in himself, and they put him on the bench. He had a couple of bad muscle pulls, too. But he is as good as he ever was."

"Do you think he could help the Giants?" Sherman asked.

"He sure as hell could. There's no receiver in the league I would rather throw to—when I'm able to throw, that is," I added with a smile. "I remember the first time I ever threw to Del in practice for the Pro Bowl game. I sent him down on a deep pattern and threw the ball with everything I had. It fell 10 yards short. He just ran right out from under it. I never had thrown to anyone with his speed. With the 49ers we had some great receivers, but nobody who could run like Shofner."

Sherman thanked me, and I returned to my room relieved that the summons had concerned Shofner and not me. A few days later I picked up the morning paper and the headline hit me right in the eyes: "Grid Giants Get Shofner!"

The trade was not only good for the team, but it was good news to me personally. Now I had a buddy who was in the same predicament as I was. Del didn't know many guys either.

When Shofner arrived at training camp, he was assigned to my room. Being West Coast rivals, we had known each other a little, and the fact that he was a fellow Texan gave us even more in common. From the moment Del showed up things began to change for the better.

Unfortunately he could not do anything to speed the healing of my injury. I continued to watch practice from the sideline— my frustration increasing daily.

On Labor Day we went to Green Bay to play the Packers, but Allie told me not to bother suiting up. It was depressing. The following week we met the Colts at the Yale Bowl, and I was still on the bench in my street clothes. But Del made a great debut with two touchdown catches and a total of 220 yards.

It was difficult for me to be out of the action as I watched Conerly get hurt early in the first period and Lee Grosscup replace him. Lee did a good job, all things considered, but Gino Marchetti and Big Daddy Lipscomb climbed all over him and gave him an intense beating. I wanted desperately to get in there and help; after all, this is why the Giants had traded for me. But there I was on the bench, beat up and out of commission.

25

Getting Ready for the Big Push

AUGUST DRAGGED ON FOR ME AT FAIRFIELD UNIVERSITY. I attended practice and squad meetings every day but began to feel again like an outsider.

Football breeds a great relationship among athletes, but you have to be in there every day banging away and getting hit to be a part of it all. You get left out if you stand on the sideline, and that's exactly how I felt—left out.

I wasn't looking for sympathy. What I was looking for was a chance to play football, but until Doc Sweeny gave me the okay to play, I was just taking up time and space. As the weeks in training camp passed, I became more and more embarrassed about my situation.

The only positive point in my life at that time was Allie Sherman. He understood my situation and knew what I was feeling.

Before becoming an NFL head coach, Sherman was the quarterback and captain of the 1941–1942 Brooklyn College football team. After graduating in 1943, he joined the Philadelphia Eagles as a quarterback and defensive back. In his rookie season he played with a combined Philadelphia Eagles and Pittsburgh Steelers squad. The team, called the Steagles, was formed due to manpower shortages caused by World War II. The team finished third in the NFL East with a record of 5–4–1. Allie was never

Allie Sherman understood my situation and knew what I was feeling.

what one would call a great quarterback, but he was a hell of a competitor just the same.

Every time Allie would sense that I was down in the dumps, he would walk over, put his arm around my shoulder, and say something like, "Just take your time, Y.A., and get ready for the big push.

We're in no hurry. We'll need you more in December than in August."

Despite the fact that Allie was only 39 years old, he had a wonderful insight into the problems of his players. He never looked upon the Giants as a team but as 40 men—each with a unique personality. Sherman realized early in his career that a successful club depended on the system adapting to the players, not the other way around. His patience and understanding made my situation easier to bear.

It had now been five weeks since I had made my debut in Los Angeles. The students at Fairfield University had returned for the fall semester and the Giants broke camp and moved to New York City, where we practiced at Fordham University. Del Shofner, Charlie Conerly, and I moved into the Concourse Plaza Hotel, which was a couple of blocks up the hill from old Yankee Stadium. Living in the city seemed to improve my spirits a little.

After the World Series ended the Giants began practicing at Yankee Stadium. Even though it was only a short walk to the ballpark, Shofner and I took the subway. To a couple of Texans like us, we got a big kick out of riding the underground railway. The first week alone, I must have ridden that rail back and forth at least a dozen times. We sure didn't have anything like it in Marshall.

The week before our opening league game with the Cardinals, things began to look up. Doc Sweeny finally gave me permission to practice. Even though my back had not completely healed, I was still able to do some light work. What a psychological lift that was for me. I ran a few plays and handled the ball. It sure felt good to be back in the game once again. It doesn't matter how much you study the playbook, there is no substitution for physical game play.

I was pretty awkward my first day at practice. I muffed the first few snaps from Ray Wietecha, the center, and my thoughts raced back to the disastrous Los Angeles game. I needed extra work on the ball exchange to improve my timing. A quarterback and center must develop precise coordination, and Ray stayed after practice to work with me.

Ray Wietecha typified the New York Giants. He was a genuine pro—dedicated. He never said much, but there wasn't a thing he didn't know about offensive-line play. After several seasons together we maneuvered the ball like a fine precision clock.

By Friday I was telling myself that maybe I would be ready for the St. Louis game on Sunday. My back finally felt good, as did my leg, and I was throwing the ball well.

I told Del to be there for me and wrote to Minnette about being able to play. Even the newspapers sensed my confidence. One featured a headline that read, "Tittle Ready—at Last!"

By Saturday morning I had completely sold myself on the idea that I would be playing against the Cardinals. I kidded Del by telling him that maybe I would throw him a couple. He laughed and cracked right back with, "It will be the first time a quarterback has thrown from the bench." Shofner was closer to the truth than he imagined.

Not only did we lose to the Cardinals 21–10, but I didn't even get into the game. Conerly opened at quarterback, but things did not go well. We looked as bad as we did against Baltimore the week before. The Cardinals were using a safety red dog. It wasn't exactly a new play, but it wasn't a common one either. Safety Larry Wilson nailed Conerly for big losses. Luke Owens dropped Charlie twice in the first period, and linebacker Bill Koman got him for minus-10 on the next series. In the second period, St. Louis defensive end Joe Rob bused through and tackled Conerly on the Giants 2. On third down, Bobby Gaiters fumbled in the end zone and Willie West recovered for a St. Louis touchdown.

During the second half of the game the Cardinals continued to hammer away at Conerly. Charlie really took a beating. His legs had given out, and he became a sitting duck for the St. Louis red-doggers.

I knew what Charlie was going through. God knows I had taken more than my share of hits. Those huge ends and tackles break through the line and hit you just as you raise your arm or maybe a linebacker shoots the gap and slams into you from the blind side. It makes you wonder where your blockers are. Each time you hit the ground, you hurt a little more and get up a little slower. You feel like saying, "The hell with this! There must be an easier way to make a living!"

The Cardinals took their toll on Conerly. Not only did they wear him down, but he began wobbling around like he was ine-

> *Each time you hit the ground, you hurt a little more and get up a little slower.*

briated. His passes lacked zip, and the ball began fluttering in the air like a bird with one wing. I saw Sherman motion to Grosscup. It was Lee's big chance, but I could not help but think it was a terrible spot for the kid. Not only were the Cardinals swarming all over us, but they had the momentum and the lead. Grosscup fared no better than Conerly.

I kept hoping that Allie would give me a shot toward the end of the game, but they were too far ahead of us by that time. The score was 21–10, and Grosscup was in trouble. I continued to walk in front of Sherman to let him know that I was there, but he ignored me.

It was neither the Giants' day nor mine.

Naturally I was disappointed about not playing, but Allie was still the coach, and I'm sure he had his reasons for not putting me in. I also realized that Sherman must have been even more disappointed than I was. This had been his first Stadium game as head coach of the Giants, and he had lost it in front of 60,000 hometown fans.

At the end of the game Allie entered the locker room and walked slowly from one locker to the next, talking quietly to each man, letting them know he still had faith in them.

When he got to where I was slumped on a stool, Sherman bent over and talked into my ear. I guess I didn't hide my disappointment as well as he did his.

"I had a reason for not sending you in there today, Y.A.," he said. "We have a 14-game schedule ahead of us. I could have used you today, but the way things went, it probably would not have done any good. And it might have done a lot of harm."

He paused and gave me a slap on the back. "One game does not make a season, Y.A. We've a long way to go. You'll be ready when the big push starts."

Allie's words made sense, and they also told me a lot about his character. Most coaches may not have played it the way he did. They would have wanted to win this one and worry about the next one next week. Truthfully, I had more or less looked at it that way myself. To me, today's game—the one *right now*—was more important than anything in the world. Win this one; never mind next week! I had played many times with painful injuries because it was important to me to win. Next Sunday always seemed too far off to worry about.

But despite my way of thinking, I was convinced Allie's decision was right. Putting me in would not have changed the course of the game or the way the Cardinals defense was shooting through there. And who knows, maybe one of those safety red-doggers might have tagged me like they did Charlie—and with my bad back, that could have been the end of my career. I soon learned that Allie Sherman was not only smart enough to make the right decisions, but he had the courage to go with them no matter how difficult they were.

The following week we went to Pittsburgh to play the Steelers, and again Conerly was the starting quarterback. I was physically ready to play but knew that Allie would be calling the shots. Whatever the call, I was ready to trust his judgment.

In the second period Charlie threw a touchdown pass to Shofner, making the score 7–7. In the third quarter we went ahead when Pat Summerall kicked a field goal, making the score 10–7. Conerly was doing a great job, and I resigned myself to another long afternoon on the bench. Grosscup had drawn the job of manning the headphones that connected to end coach Ken Kavanaugh in the scouting booth upstairs. I had nothing to do except watch the game.

All of a sudden Charlie was in trouble. Two big Steelers linemen—Lou Michaels and Joe Krupa—broke through the line and belted Conerly for a six-yard loss. Charlie was visibly shaken by the hits. On the next play Big Daddy Lipscomb slammed his 290-pound body into Charlie and dropped him seven yards behind the line of scrimmage. Conerly was having trouble getting up.

Conerly was having trouble getting up.

Allie waved for Kyle Rote to call a timeout. The trainers ran on to the field to see if Charlie was okay.

"Start warming up, Y.A.!" yelled Sherman. "You're going in for Conerly."

I flew off the bench and grabbed for a football. All of a sudden I began to worry about my back. I still was not sure I could throw long. I had been preparing myself for this moment for the past six weeks, but I was unexplainably filled with doubt. After throwing a few warm-up passes, my confidence began to return. I told myself that this was my shot and to make it a good one!

I could feel a sense of uncertainty when I entered the huddle. I was stepping into Charlie Conerly's shoes, something no other quarterback had been able to do. I knew that the next few minutes would decide my future as the Giants' quarterback, and so did the players in the huddle.

I decided to play it close to the vest until I got the feel of things. Sherman always told me to go with the percentage shots, and that's exactly what I did. My target would be Shofner.

With first down on the Pittsburgh 42, I passed 12 yards to Del on a square-out pattern. Next I hit him on a quick slant for a first down on the Steelers 18. Again I passed to him over the middle, and we were on the 5-yard line. It was then time to run the ball. I tried handing off to Alex Webster around right end, but Michaels stopped him for no gain. On second down I used Shofner as a decoy left and passed to Joe Morrison on a swing pattern to the right for the touchdown.

I had thrown many touchdowns in my career, but none had given me such a thrill. I was overjoyed. I had come in for Conerly and had taken *his* Giants in for the score.

The Giants defense continued to hold off the Steelers, and we won the game 17–14. I finished off the day with 10 completions in 12 tries for 123 yards. I hit my first six passes in a row on that first scoring march.

Sitting in a crowded dressing room at Pitt Stadium, I was the happiest guy in the world. My back and groin had held out despite some healthy licks in the last period. I was finally a decent quarterback again.

26

Sharing the Quarterback Position

AS USUAL THE MEDIA HAD TO SENSATIONALIZE THE NEW YORK win over Pittsburgh. One newspaper went so far as to call my performance against the Steelers, "the beginning of a new era for the Giants." Now how can a man's value to a team be based on one ballgame? No one knew better than I that the next timeout I might get hurt or be a bum—or, just as easily, Charlie Conerly could be the hero. Nothing bothered me more than seeing references suggesting that Charlie was on his way out. It was unfair. The sportswriters seemed to forget that Charlie had given the Giants a 10–7 lead before I had gotten into the game.

This situation was not new to me. The only difference this time was that I was on the other side of the fence. Usually it was some other quarterback who had a hot game that put old Y.A. on the bench.

When we returned to practice at Fordham on Tuesday there was a cloud of uneasiness in the air. That morning Sherman came out to the field and told Charlie and me that he wanted to see us in his office. He didn't say why, but Conerly and I already knew. Allie had been visibly upset by the situation.

Allie's office at Fordham was a small, cluttered room that was shared by other members of his staff. It had three or four old

metal lockers against one wall and a desk and blackboard opposite the lockers. A couple of showers were situated in the small
room that adjoined the office. Boxes and crates were piled all
over the place. I wondered how a coach could operate in such
horrid conditions.

Sherman asked Ken Kavanaugh and Ed Koman to leave. He
closed the door behind them, turned toward us, and referred
briefly to the newspaper speculations.

"Fellows, I asked to see you this morning because there is
something which needs saying. I want to say it now. I would
not be talking like this to any other quarterbacks in the league,
but I feel you two are mature enough and have been around
long enough to appreciate the ticklish position we are in. You
have both been starting quarterbacks for years, but now I must
ask you to make sacrifices and put your faith in me. I will be
making a lot of moves and, barring injury, there will never be a
time when one of you aren't playing. It isn't going to be easy for
any of us, but it will be a lot harder if we do not have complete
understanding."

Both Charlie and I nodded in agreement. Allie continued.

"This can be very good or it can be very bad. Working with
two quarterbacks is difficult, but we can make it work because
I have faith in you men. I hope you have faith in me. There will
be things in the press and comments from people even closer
to the ballclub. Some may be nasty things that can tear us apart
if we let 'em, but I will tell you right now, you are both No. 1
with Al Sherman, no matter who starts. Remember this, and
we can do it, the three of us. If you have anything to say let's
hear it now. Once we walk out that door, I will consider the
matter closed."

Conerly scraped his cleats on the rough wooden floor and without looking up, said, "Hell, Al, I have had my share of good years. I don't care who starts as long as we win this thing."

I was glad to see this reaction from Charlie. I felt the same way and let it be known to Allie.

With a sigh of relief, Sherman shook Charlie's hand and then mine.

"You're real men," he said. "And with men like you, we *can* win it all!"

This was the kind of thing that made playing with the Giants special. They developed a warm and human relationship that included players, coaches, and front office. It was something I had seldom felt on other ballclubs. The Giants treated every athlete like an individual, like a man. You always knew where you stood.

From that day on, the expression "No. 1 quarterback" was never again used by Sherman or anyone else connected with the organization.

> The Giants treated every athlete like an individual, like a man.

Charlie and I went along, knowing we both would play a lot of football. It was going to be a long season, and there would be chances for both of us. Neither of us was a kid, nor were we looking ahead to a brand-new career. Charlie was 40, and I was 35. We both wanted a championship—me especially. I had never played in a championship game, and it was getting late.

Allie had asked us to have faith in him the day we had our closed-door meeting at Fordham. Now Charlie needed that same faith the very next Sunday!

The Giants took the train down to Washington to meet the Redskins in the first game ever played in the new D.C. Stadium. The Redskins fumbled the opening kickoff, and we recovered.

Conerly took the club right in for a score, passing 17 yards to Kyle Rote for the touchdown. He made it look easy.

But just as quickly, the tide changed. Washington stormed back and tied the score when Norm Snead passed to Don Bosseler in the end zone.

Then came the play that almost destroyed us. With the ball on the Giants' 45, Conerly underthrew Shofner on a long pass, and the ball went straight into the hands of Dale Hackbart, the Washington defensive back. He ran it back 48 yards for a touchdown. We were behind almost as quickly as we had gone ahead.

Sherman had told me a few minutes earlier to start warming up. After Hackbart's interception, Allie waved me in to the game and called Conerly to the sideline.

Charlie was really upset. He thought Sherman had pulled him out of the game because of the interception. It was the first time I ever saw Conerly really angry. He stormed past Allie, slammed his helmet into the ground, and sat at the far end of the bench.

He stormed past Allie, slammed his helmet into the ground, and sat at the far end of the bench.

Everyone was well aware of the tension and seemed to be waiting for another spark to ignite the flame, but it had all been resolved in the dressing room before we boarded the Pennsylvania Railroad headed for New York.

As for me, I finished the game that day, and we beat the Redskins 24–21. I was still a little uncertain of the Giants' offense, so I stuck with passes. I threw screens, flares, and short patterns. In all, I threw the football 41 times and completed 24 for 315 yards.

27

The 1961 NFL Eastern Division Championship

THE SKY WAS DARK ABOVE YANKEE STADIUM, but the score-board lights shone brightly against the December afternoon. From the Giants' bench across the field, I could read, "Cleveland 7, New York 7."

My eyes quickly shifted toward the clock. There were two minutes left—120 seconds away from winning the NFL Eastern Division championship. The Giants had gone into this final game of 1961 needing only a win or a tie against Cleveland to clinch the title. All we had to do was hang on for a while longer, and the championship was ours.

But the Browns had Bobby Mitchell at flanker. Mitchell was a threat, no matter how much time was left. Bobby, one of the fastest men in pro football, could bust a game wide open in one shot. He had done it plenty of times before.

I was sitting on the bench next to Charlie Conerly. We had failed to make a first down on our last series, and Allie Sherman had sent the punting team in to the game. The ball was on the Giants' 35 as Don Chandler dropped back to kick.

"Damn, I hope he puts this one out of here," I said to Conerly.

"If anyone can, it's Chandler," said Charlie. "He's the best pressure kicker in the league."

Just then Don swung his leg, and his foot exploded against the ball. The ball spiraled up and up, and for a moment it seemed to disappear into the black sky.

Mitchell was back there waiting for the ball on the 30. If he had gotten his hands on it, we would have been in trouble, but he didn't. The ball sailed far over his head. He backpedaled hard, trying to reach the ball, but Chandler had gunned it 70 yards— too far for anyone to catch.

By the time Bobby could pick up the ball on a bounce, Bob Simms, the Giants' fine rookie linebacker, darted out in front of him and downed it on the Cleveland 7.

Chandler's great punt had sealed the Browns' fate. Mitchell was stopped by Sam Huff on a couple of end runs, and then a long pass from Milt Plum to Mitchell fell short. Sam Baker punted, and we took over. Sherman sent Conerly in to kill the clock, and I just sat there trying to make the time go faster. There were 15 seconds left when Charlie ran the ball into the line on a quarterback sneak.

That very moment I experienced one of the greatest thrills of my football career. As the clock ran down to 10 seconds left, the huge crowd in Yankee Stadium started to chant, "Ten, nine, eight…"

The chanting got louder and louder as it echoed around the ballpark like thunder.

> *The chanting got louder and louder as it echoed around the ballpark like thunder.*

"Seven, six, five, four…"

In all my years of playing professional football, I had never been a part of anything like this. I threw off my cold-weather cape, jumped to my feet, and joined the fans as they shouted off the last few seconds.

"Three, two, one…"

The final gun sounded with a bang! The game was over, and a roar went up from the stands. I jumped around like a schoolboy, shaking hands and slapping everyone on the back. It was my first time with a championship team. I flung my helmet into the air and then realized that I could have killed someone if it had hit them on the head, but luckily for me no one seemed to mind. The Giants bench had become bedlam.

It was a good half hour after the game had ended before I began to unwind. I did not realize how tired I was, both mentally and physically, until I sat down in front of my locker and began removing my jersey.

It had been a long year, but looking back the 1961 season with New York gave me my greatest thrill in football. Personally, I don't think it was my finest season because I had better years with San Francisco in 1953 and 1957 and with Baltimore in 1948. But this was definitely the most *satisfying* season because so many people, especially the 49ers, had written me off. But now, after 13 years, I was a winner and would be playing in the *big one* for the first time.

New York City became a wonderland for me after we won the '61 Eastern Division championship. I won a Chrysler car and was named to the Associated Press and United Press International All-Pro teams. I was the recipient of the Jim Thorpe Award as the MVP in professional football—an award voted on by the players themselves. Then, to top it off, I received a phone call from Arthur Poretz, a New York public-relations man, who informed me that I had won the Howard Clothes Award as the most popular Giant. Poretz said over half a million New York fans had voted in the contest.

"I'm honored, Art," I said. "What is the award?"

"A yacht," he said.

I couldn't believe my ears! "A *what*?" I asked.

Poretz laughed. "It's a 30-foot cabin cruiser, Y.A."

"But I'm not a yachtsman," I said.

"You are now!"

I would have traded it all to beat the Packers for the title, but we ran into a great football team in Green Bay that year. They kicked the hell out of us, 37–0. They were definitely the better team, and there was no denying it.

The game was played on December 30, 1961, in front of 39,029 screaming Packers fans. On the first play of the second quarter, halfback Paul Hornung, who set a championship-game scoring record with 19 points, went in for a touchdown. Next Bart Starr passed to Boyd Dowler for another score a few minutes after Ray Nitschke intercepted one of my throws. The score was 14–0 right off the bat.

If we had any hopes of catching up, they were quickly diminished on the next series of downs. On the first play from our 32, I had Rote and Shofner wide open on a deep pass pattern. But before I could get rid of the ball, Willie Davis, the big Packer defensive end, crashed into me from the blind side and sacked me for a loss. On the next play I tried a screen pass to Alex Webster, but he could not get open. I was forced to throw to my second man, Joe Walton. The pass was incomplete. On third down, Rote beat Hank Gremminger on a deep route, but I underthrew Kyle badly, and the ball went right into the hands of the Packers defensive back.

Green Bay capitalized on the Gremminger interception and scored once again. This sealed the Giants' fate.

The locker room was an awful sight. Everyone, except Conerly, showed the emotional strain of the embarrassing defeat. As always, his expression gave no clue as to what he really felt inside.

But no one felt the loss more deeply than Allie Sherman. Even though his eyes were moist and he was flushed with anger and humiliation, he refused to let the game get him down. He jumped up on the table in the middle of the crowded locker room and hollered for attention.

"Now I know how tough this thing is," he said, and the bitterness of the moment hung on his words. "But let me tell you this. You are Giants, and when you walk out that door, you're going to walk out with your heads held high. You're going to look them in the eye. You are not going to look ashamed or beaten."

Rosey Grier, the 300-pound defensive tackle, growled, "Damn right, Allie."

Then Sherman said, "We have been whipped before, and we'll get whipped again. But don't let this one get you down. We will be back again. We have had a great season, and I am proud to have been your coach. Now square those shoulders and walk tall. Good-bye and thank you."

During my flight home to San Francisco, I wondered if I would get another chance at the title. For that matter, I wondered if I would be back in a Giants uniform in 1962.

28

Frank Gifford: The Comeback Kid

RETURNING TO SAN FRANCISCO IN 1962 WEARING A GIANTS uniform was something less than triumphant.

The Giants flew to the West Coast from Fairfield University in August to play the 49ers in our first exhibition game. Naturally I was mighty excited at the prospect of playing in Kezar Stadium against my former ballclub.

The year before the 49ers had written me off and said I was washed up as a quarterback. Now I was returning as the NFL's MVP and a member of the team that had won the Eastern Division championship in 1961. What a difference a year had made!

I was anxious to play well in front of my old fans, but it did not turn out that way. Both the Giants and I played poorly, and San Francisco damn near ran us out of Kezar. The final score was 42–10—quite a humiliation for me, personally.

Even though it was only an exhibition game, I took the loss hard. Playing poorly in my old ballpark was a bitter experience for me. It was important that I win for the Giants, but there were personal reasons, too. Red Hickey had traded me because he thought I was through as a quarterback. I wanted to prove him wrong.

Playing poorly in my old ballpark was a bitter experience for me.

After the game, I sat in the locker room for 20 minutes before taking off my jersey and pads. Finally I got up and walked over to where Frank Gifford was dressing.

"By golly, Frank, I do not see how we can win this thing again. Look at what those guys did to us out there today. They murdered us!"

"Oh, we are going to win, Y.A., don't worry about that," Gifford replied confidently.

But I still wasn't satisfied.

"How are we going to win it?" I asked. "Rote and Conerly have both retired. Pat Summerall is gone, and Livingston has been traded. And how about you, Frank? You've been trying to make a comeback, and you have been hurting ever since you got to camp. How the hell are you going to do it?"

"Listen, Y.A.," he said firmly. "We will win this thing because we always win!"

"But how?" I asked, wanting more reassurance.

"I don't know how," he replied, "but just mark my words. We are going to win."

Gifford reflected the Giants' general attitude. He always approached a ballgame with the enthusiasm and desire of a rookie. He prepared and worked hard, believe me. In training camp he drove himself to the limit—both physically and mentally. There was never any *halfway* with Frank. His greatness was no accident. He laid the groundwork all week, and every move was directed at a single purpose: winning the game like we had always won it!

This was the same confidence that the team had in its own ability, its own destiny. It's what made it different from any team I had ever played with. The team always went into a season with no doubt of winning it all. Gifford, Huff, and Webster believed it. They also knew it would be a struggle, and the struggle began sooner than anyone expected.

We lost two of our first five games. First Cleveland beat us in the opener 17–7, and then Pittsburgh squeaked by 20–17. Our record was 3–2 going into our game with the Detroit Lions at Yankee Stadium.

If the 1962 season had a turning point, it was that October 21 game against the Lions. A loss to Detroit would have dropped us to .500. This was a must-win game against a tough Lions team. Their guys on defense were big, not to mention strong. Sam Williams and Darris McCord played at end, and Roger Brown and Alex Karras were at tackle. Middle linebacker Joe Schmidt was terrific. This defense was the best in the league in 1962.

Despite all this power, Allie Sherman told us, "We will run on them, and we will pass on them."

His battle plan was simple: "Nobody runs straight at Karras and Brown and the rest of those big boys. They are always trying to run slants and sweeps with fancy angle blocking. But that is not the way. You've got to beat those front four guys head-to-head. You can't pussyfoot around them. That is what we will do Sunday. We will take the ball and run it straight at them. We will not look for the easy way. We will beat them right up front, man-to-man, and we will win the game!"

That Sunday our offensive line slugged it out with the Detroit defense every yard of the way. Rosey Brown, at 260 pounds, had a great duel with the 6'5", 250-pound Lions' end, Sam Williams. Six-foot Giants guard Darrell Dess collided with 6'5", 300-pound Roger Brown and moved the Lion tackle out of the way when needed. It was really something to see! Every yard gained that day was earned.

I stayed with Sherman's pregame plan. Phil King and Alex Webster ran the ball straight at the Lions on quick traps and dive plays. Then, when we had Detroit thinking that we were going to run, we would throw the ball. Not long, but effectively—just enough to keep them honest.

The Lions scored early on a 48-yard pass from Milt Plum to Gail Cogdill. But we took the kickoff and controlled the ball for almost eight minutes, moving down to the Lions' 4-yard line. With a first down, I figured they would be expecting a power play into the line; we had been having success with King and Webster inside the tackles. So I faked Webster left, and bootlegged the ball around the right end for a touchdown. As I crossed the goal line, Dick "Night Train" Lane, the Lions halfback, hit me with a solid shot to the helmet. I went down hard. I was shaken up but able to walk off the field under my own power.

On the sideline, Sherman asked me if I was okay, and I said yes.

I had been knocked dizzy in ballgames before and was not overly concerned over his incident. But then a funny thing happened. Allie called me off the bench to discuss a defense the Lions were using.

"When they go into that setup, Y.A.," he said, "your best automatic call would be a 34."

"A 34?" I asked. "You know we don't have a 34-automatic, Allie."

Sherman's eyes popped open. The 34-automatic was one of our standard plays. I had been using it for two years, and here I was telling him that we had no such play.

"Are you sure you're all right?" he inquired again.

"What makes you ask?"

"You got hit pretty hard in the head. Maybe it shook you up more than you know."

I told Allie that I was feeling fine. Then, all of a sudden, things got fuzzy. I couldn't remember a thing—not a single play, not a single pass call. I did not even know how to set a formation. Physically I felt okay, but my mind was completely blank!

Doc Sweeny had me sit down on the bench. He asked me what my name was.

I couldn't remember a thing—not a single play, not a single pass call.

"Y.A. Tittle," I said. "You know damned well what my name is, Doc."

"Sure I do, Y.A.," he said. "But I wanted to see if you did."

Then Doc asked me, "Who are we playing today?"

"Detroit."

I could have told Doc the score, the down, and everything else that was going on, but I could not remember one single Giants play or formation!

I remained on the bench the entire first half not knowing what had happened to me. At halftime I went in to the dressing room and all of a sudden my head had cleared. I could remember again. Boy, was I relieved! I ran over to Sherman and yelled, "You're right, Allie, we do have a 34-automatic. Great play, too."

I got back into the game in the second half. King scored a touchdown in the third period from a yard out to tie the score at 14–14, then Don Chandler kicked a nine-yard field goal for the win. We beat Detroit 17–14.

Our next game was against Washington, and they were unbeaten. The Redskins were on a hot streak thanks to Norm Snead's passing and the catching of Bobby Mitchell, who had come from Cleveland in a trade. The Skins came to town leading the Eastern Division with a record of 4–0–2.

That Sunday—October 28, 1962—turned out to be the greatest day I ever had in pro football. I threw seven touchdown passes to tie the NFL record shared by Sid Luckman of the Chicago Bears and Adrian Burk, my former Baltimore teammate. I completed 27 of 39 for 505 yards. We beat Washington 49–34.

We played Dallas on December 16. That day I set a league record with my 33rd touchdown pass of the year—my second-greatest thrill of 1962—but it was anticlimactic. The Giants had clinched the division title two weeks earlier with a 26–24 decision over the Chicago Bears. The 41–31 victory over Dallas and a 17–13 win over Cleveland were merely icing on the cake.

As Gifford had told me, "We always win."

The season that had opened on such a disappointing note in San Francisco ended in grand fashion with the Giants winning the Eastern Division for the second straight year.

As Gifford had told me, "We always win."

29

Beat the Packers!

THE GIANTS' KICKER, DON CHANDLER, KICKED A LOT OF BIG field goals in 1962, but his biggest was a 16-yarder that beat the Bears 26–24.

It sealed the Eastern Division championship but also turned our thoughts to another showdown with the Packers. The memory of the 37–0 beating they had given us a year earlier was still fresh. We wanted another shot at them, and this was our chance at a rematch...well, possibly a rematch. As I recall, Green Bay had not yet won the Western Division title, but it was only a matter of time. The Lions would be the only team to beat them throughout the '62 season.

The week before the game, the city of New York was a football madhouse. Championship fever was everywhere. Green Bay was the heavy favorite, but I felt we had a better chance than in 1961. I wanted this one badly, because now I was the Giants' *only* quarterback—the year prior I had shared the job with Charlie Conerly.

I really thought we could do it, and so did the rest of the team. There was an intensity about them that I had never seen before. The defense was really worked up.

If the New York defense could have played offense on Sunday, December 30, we might have won the championship. Andy Robustelli and his gang played superbly. The defensive effort was one of the best I had ever seen, but as in 1961, our offense could not move the ball. The Packers beat us once again, 16–7.

It was a bitter-cold day, and the icy wind that swept through Yankee Stadium at better than 40 mph made it seem even colder than 17 degrees. By the time I threw my second pass in the pregame warm-up drill, my fingers were frozen stiff and I could hardly hold the football. The wind ripped through my uniform and stung me from head to toe.

By the time I threw my second pass in the pregame warm-up drill, my fingers were frozen stiff.

Although the Giants were primarily a passing team in 1962, Sherman's game play for Green Bay called for us to take the ball to them on the ground. We wanted to establish our running game. We were going to take on the Packers' defense— Willie Davis, Hawg Hanner, Henry Jordan, and Bill Quinlan. We were going to run it down their throats, wear them out.

The wind was blowing up a storm, which made the day better suited for running. Green Bay was basically a rushing team. The Packers' fullback, Jimmy Taylor, carried the ball 31 times that day and gained almost as much yardage by himself as the entire Giants backfield.

Despite the adverse conditions, we still almost won the game. Our defense did a tremendous job and, with a few breaks, things could have gone our way. What do I mean by breaks? I'll tell you. Sam Huff and Robustelli and the rest of our defensive guys hit Taylor and the Green Bay backs so hard that they fumbled five times. But five times the ball bounced right to some Packer who happened to be standing in the right place at the right time. We fumbled twice, Phil King on a run and Sam Horner on a punt, and Ray Nitschke recovered both for the Packers.

The Giants' defense could not be faulted for the defeat. Robustelli and his boys were mean and aggressive. They gave Taylor the treatment on every play. Three or four of them hit Jimmy every time he came through or around the line. They drove into him and flattened him on the frozen ground. The Packers fullback was charged with three of the five fumbles. Paul Hornung fumbled once along with teammate Tom Moore.

After the game Green Bay quarterback Bart Starr said, "It was terrible. The huddle would form and we would watch Taylor come back after Huff and Katcavage [and the rest of them] had hit him. He would be bent over holding his insides together. I never saw a back get such a beating!"

"It was the only play of the game they didn't touch me," said Taylor of his and Green Bay's only touchdown. "But they sure made up for it the rest of the time. It was the toughest game of my life. They really came to play!"

The break that hurt us the most was Horner's fumble of a punt by Max McGee in the middle of the third quarter. The Packers were leading 10–7, but we had our defense in high gear. With the ball on the Green Bay 33, Taylor tried a sweep and Rosey Grier decked him for a yard loss. Jim then tried the left side, and Dick Modzelewski flattened him for another loss. Then Starr's pass to Ron Kramer was incomplete—thanks to a vicious rush by Robustelli. McGee was now forced to punt on fourth down. The kick was low, and Horner had to kneel to catch it, but in doing so he fumbled the ball and Nitschke recovered for the Packers. A few minutes later Jerry Kramer kicked a field goal, and the score was 13–7. It was also the beginning of the end for the Giants.

Nitschke had been a pain in the ass all day. In the first half I had Joe Walton wide open in the end zone, but Ray deflected the ball as it left my hand. It hung there for a second and it came straight down to Dan Currie (another Packers linebacker), who ran it up to the 50. I can still see Walton all alone in the end zone waving at me to get the ball to him. It was a sure touchdown.

The biggest problem of the day for both teams was the weather. I doubt if any quarterback could have thrown well in that wind. The frozen ground kept backs like Shofner and Rote from breaking loose when trying to catch the ball. The ice did not allow for traction. Instead of running, they just skidded on the ice.

I had two shots at the big one and came up empty-handed both times.

So that's how it was in my first two championship games as a Giant. I had two shots at the big one and came up empty-handed both times.

30

Never Winning the Big One

"TITTLE DOESN'T WIN THE BIG ONES!"

This is something I have lived with for a long time. They said it when I was with San Francisco in 1957 when we lost the Western Division playoff to Detroit after leading 24–10 at the half. And they said it again in 1961 and 1962 when the Packers beat us for the title. But I hoped that this time would be different. After all, the Giants' 1963 season record was 11–3—our only losses coming to the Steelers, the Browns, and the Cardinals. Once again we were Eastern Division champs and ready to take on the Chicago Bears for the league championship.

The week leading up to the Chicago game was an experience I will never forget. Frank Gifford started it all by interviewing me on a CBS television show. It was based on the old *This Is Your Life* show, but this was more like *This Is Your Life, Y.A. Tittle*. After the show was over, everyone in New York City knew that I lived in Eastchester. My phone wasn't unlisted and therefore rang day and night with well-wishers wishing me luck against Chicago. If the phone wasn't ringing, the doorbell was. People were coming over to get my autograph and say, "Go get 'em, Y.A!"

One morning I found a parking ticket on my car. As I removed it from the windshield, I noticed that there was some writing on the back. It read, "Forget the ticket, Y.A., just beat the Bears!" Even the Eastchester Police Department was rooting for me. My two boys, Pat and Mike, attended the Immaculate Conception school in Eastchester. Even though we were not Catholics, the nuns were great to my kids. One nun, Sister Marguerite, said the Rosary for me every day leading up to the game. The entire school was praying for the Giants.

The entire school was praying for the Giants.

The Chicago defense had size and experience, but any defense can be controlled. There wasn't a defensive man in the league who could cover man-to-man on Shofner or someone like him if he didn't have help in that secondary and if the pass was thrown correctly. The 14-yard touchdown pass I threw to Gifford in the first quarter was an example of that. Frank worked on Chicago halfback Bennie McRae for a couple of plays and then told me in the huddle, "Y.A., I can beat him easy on a zig-out." So I threw a zig-out off play action, and Gifford easily beat him for the touchdown.

There was only one problem; just as I got rid of the ball, Larry Morris blitzed through and hit me across the left leg. I felt a twinge behind my knee. I walked it off and then went back into the game. I could feel that there was something wrong. I said to Kyle Rote, "I hope I can last this out. My knee is starting to get stiff."

My knee held out until late in the second quarter. The Bears had scored after Morris intercepted one of my passes and ran 61 yards, but Don Chandler had kicked a field goal, keeping the score in our favor, 10–7.

We had the ball on the Chicago 32—first and 10. I dropped back to pass to Gifford, but I stumbled on the hard ground and fell as I got rid of the ball. Again, Morris came crashing through the line and dove onto my bad knee. This time the pain shot clear up my leg. It was like someone had stuck a knife in the knee joint. I could hardly limp off the field. This time I knew it was bad.

I was taken to the dressing room, and Doc Sweeny and Dr. Anthony Pisani, an orthopedist, took a look at my knee.

"It's killing me," I told them. "I can't even bend it."

Dr. Pisani asked me where the pain was, and I pointed to the spot. He froze it with a spray and then gave me a needle. I don't know what it was, and at the time I didn't give a damn. I was too busy cussing my luck. When the guys came in at the half, I acted as though it wasn't that bad. I didn't want them to see me looking as bad as I felt.

I knew the team was concerned about my condition, so before they went out for the second half I said, "I don't know if I can play on this damned thing. But even if I can't, I am convinced we can whip these guys. We're ahead now. We can stay there."

Once out on the field, I began to throw some warm-up passes behind the bench. Sherman asked me, "How does it feel, Y.A.? What do you think?"

"It could be worse, Al, but let me give it a whirl."

A couple of warm-up passes told me I was severely handicapped. I couldn't drop straight back to pass; I was forced to backpedal, which made me a lot slower. But on our first series I came up against a third-and-7 situation and had no choice but to throw the ball. I called a Green Bay special—one of our favorite patterns— and dropped back to throw to Morrison in the flat. Joe made a first down. *Hot damn, maybe I can do it after all,* I thought.

The thought was short-lived. On the next play I overshot Gifford on a sideline square-out pattern. He was wide open waiting for the ball, but I couldn't plant on my front left knee, and my pass was late. The next pass was intended for Shofner, but I was intercepted. Later that period I tried a screen pass to the right and Ed O'Bradovich, the Bears' defensive end, intercepted it and ran it down near our goal line. Bill Wade scored for Chicago on short yardage, making the score 14–10, Bears.

I was still putting the ball in the air in the fourth quarter, but it was no use. The Bears knew I had to throw and they were dropping everyone but George Halas into the secondary to cover my receivers. They knew darn well that, because of my knee, I couldn't put any zip on my passes. The ball was wobbling end-over-end, and there was nothing I could do about it.

The game ended when Richie Petitbon intercepted a pass in the end zone. I had been aiming it at Gifford, but it never got there.

I had lost another "big one."

I never felt lower than I did at that moment. No defeat had ever been as hard to take. In the dressing room I eased my aching body on to a stool and cried. Gifford's locker was next to mine and he, too, was wiping away the tears.

Sherman walked over to both Frank and me. He put his arm on my shoulder and whispered, "Y.A., you're still the greatest. We had them today. You had them. It's not your fault. I know how much you wanted this one. I wanted it, too, but there will be other chances for both you and me."

He then put his hand on Gifford's shoulder and whispered something to him. Frank was still leaning against the locker with his face to the wall. His body was shaking, and I knew he was terribly upset.

Well the Bears had beaten us, and we had lost the championship three years in a row. All around the league they began to chant, "Tittle doesn't win the big ones!" Maybe so, but I knew that the guys who sang this tune were usually home *watching* the big one on TV. Thanks to Allie Sherman and a great Giants team, I *played* in them.

31

The End of an Era

WHILE 1963 HAD BEEN MY BEST SEASON STATISTICALLY, 1964 became one of my worst. Allie Sherman had swept out his aging stars all at once, and their replacements just didn't jell—especially on defense. I don't think anyone could have foreseen what was to happen to the Giants.

We opened the season with two straight losses—something that was totally uncharacteristic of our team. Our first game was played at Philadelphia, and the Eagles killed us 38–7. The second game was against the Steelers in Pittsburgh. For the first three quarters it looked like the Giants would prevail, but we let it get away from us in the fourth quarter and ended up losing 24–27. It was also a turning point for me in my professional career.

Morris Berman, a photographer with the *Pittsburgh Post-Gazette* snapped a photo of me immediately after I had been savagely blindsided by 270-pound defensive end John Baker of the Pittsburgh Steelers. The photo shows me kneeling in the end zone, shoulders drooped and arms resting on my thighs. I have a dazed look in my eyes and blood trickling down the side of my head.

Baker had crushed the cartilage in my ribs and brutally gashed my forehead, knocking off my helmet. I also suffered a concussion and a cracked sternum. That photo would later become one of the most enduring images in sports history. What a hell of a way to get famous!

Years later Baker used this photo in his campaign to win election as the first African American sheriff in North Carolina's Wake County—a position he held for 24 years. He put my picture on his campaign posters that said, "If you don't obey the law, this is what Big John will do to you!"

At home the following week we barely beat the Redskins, 13–10. This was our third game of the season, and I had thrown only one touchdown in three games. By that time the previous year I had already thrown six.

For the next three weeks, things only got worse. The Giants' offense was virtually nonexistent. We gained less than 200 yards of total offense in a game and turned the ball over nine times. We had lost to both the Lions and the Eagles and tied Dallas. Our record was a miserable 1–4–1.

For the next three weeks, things only got worse.

In our seventh game the six turnovers against Cleveland didn't help matters. They were one of the strongest teams in the league and ended up crushing us 42–20.

Finally, on November 1, the Giants came to life. With only one turnover, we were able to dominate the Cardinals. I threw four touchdown passes, and we beat St. Louis 34–17.

But the exhilaration of the win was unfortunately short-lived. We lost to Dallas, tied St. Louis, and then lost to Pittsburgh and Minnesota. In our final game of the season we were annihilated by the Browns 52–20.

We fell to last place and finished the season with a 2–10–2 record…the worst in Giants history.

A few weeks later I announced my retirement before a jammed press conference at Momma Leone's. I told the reporters that I didn't want to come back and be a mediocre football player. That same day another press conference was being held at Toots Shor's restaurant. The New York Jets showed up with their young new quarterback—a guy by the name of Joe Namath.

A few years later I met up with Frank Gifford and we talked about my retirement. I told him to put himself in my place. You struggle year after year, then all of a sudden your unbelievable dreams come true. You're playing winning ball in front of 62,000 people in the House That Ruth Built, you're on *The Ed Sullivan Show*, and you're being called upon to endorse products and make commercials; then all of a sudden you're 38—an old man—and the door slams shut behind you. But you know something? For 27 years, every time the center gave me the ball, I chuckled. *Dadgummit*, I thought, *I've got hold of it again!*

Fourth Quarter

Life after Football

32

Civilian Life

AFTER RETIREMENT MINNETTE AND I TRAVELED THE WORLD extensively. We still do. When I'm not traveling or visiting my other home in Sedona, Arizona, I'm still involved with my insurance business. My son John has now taken over.

I have been in the insurance business since 1955. It all started with me traveling door-to-door selling insurance. Over the years, due to its success and aided by the phenomenal growth of the Silicon Valley, my company has grown to be one of the top three largest broker businesses in Northern California.

Director Oliver Stone cast me as one of the opposing coaches in the 1999 movie Any Given Sunday.

I also dabbled in films. Director Oliver Stone cast me as one of the opposing coaches in the 1999 movie *Any Given Sunday.* Four other Hall of Fame players made cameo appearances as opposing head coaches—Bob St. Clair, Dick Butkus, Warren Moon, and Johnny Unitas. I was in very good company!

33

The Hall of Fame

BEING ENSHRINED INTO THE PRO FOOTBALL HALL OF FAME in Canton, Ohio, was the greatest thrill of my life. I was notified of this honor in February 1971 and was asked to select a presenter. As I contemplated this task, I came to the decision that the person I would select would have to be a good friend and love the game of football as much as I do. I chose New York Giants owner Wellington Mara. Wellington not only loved football, he loved his team and the players too.

Being enshrined into the Pro Football Hall of Fame in Canton, Ohio, was the greatest thrill of my life.

That hot August day in Canton was the first time in the history of the enshrinement that the same man would present two members of the same class. Wellington presented both Vince Lombardi and myself. What an honor!

I spoke highly of the men who molded me into an NFL quarterback—my father, who sincerely believed that I could play high school football; Otis Mitchell, my high school coach, who gave me confidence and taught me technique; the late Bernie Moore, who convinced me that I was good enough to be a pro; and Cecil Isbell, who truly believed that I was the greatest passer that he had ever seen…well, at least he convinced *me* of that. Two other people who were great inspirations to me during my pro football career were San Francisco 49ers quarterback Frankie Albert and 49ers head coach Buck Shaw.

Standing on that stage and being honored with the other great men from the Class of 1971—my Giants teammate Andy Robustelli, Norm Van Brocklin, Frank "Bruiser" Kinard, Bill Hewitt, the great Jim Brown, and coach Vince Lombardi—was an extremely humbling experience.

It was a day I will never forget.

34

Reflections

AS FOR THE GAME TODAY, WELL, IT HAS CHANGED QUITE A BIT. The rules have created that, and the game is now wide open. A player can now use his hands when pass-blocking. My right tackle and Hall of Fame colleague Bob St. Clair didn't have the luxury of using his hands to pass-block. He wasn't supposed to, but he did it anyway. And he got away with it most of the time.

I don't think that the game has changed for the better. I don't like the free-substitution rules, where you can send in six, seven, or eight players at a time. Sometimes I don't even know who is in the game. Having four or five people coming in and out on every down can be really confusing. Today's fans don't get the opportunity to develop a favorite player. Players in my era had distinctive and separate personalities. The fans knew them because they played every down.

> *I don't think that the game has changed for the better.*

I liked the game that was played in the 1950s and 1960s much more than I like today's game. In the past we did our own thing, and quarterbacks called their own plays with the help of their teammates on the field.

In today's game they have some guy in the press box with three or four assistants. They sit there with a battery of television monitors watching every down situation. They then send the play down to the coach, who relays it to the quarterback, and he repeats what the people upstairs said.

When the game is over, can you say that the quarterback called a bad game? No, you can't, because he didn't make the call; the people upstairs did! Can the sportswriters say that the quarterback "threw wildly today"? Maybe he did it because the guys weren't open. And it really wasn't his fault because maybe the play selection was poor. The sportswriters criticize the players when they don't even know who is calling the plays. I don't like it, but that's the system.

I enjoyed my era because I could be my own boss. I liked to do things my way because I knew what I could do well and not so well. I was a good outside passer because I could hit people outside. I could hit deep corners or deep sideline, anything that was one-on-one.

The camaraderie in the golden era was the last of its kind. It was a continuation of the generations that came before. Back then we did it—the 11 guys on offense and the 11 guys on defense—not so much the coaches. Our coaches prepared us for the game, but on game day the game was mostly turned over to the players.

I was a product of the final era in professional football—before the big salaries, expansion teams, and big money. I was so fortunate to have played in football's golden age—a time filled with so many great players. The good friends I made through football are friends to this day. I wouldn't trade the time I played for any other era in professional football.

APPENDIX I

Tittle's Career, Season by Season

1948

In 1948 the Cleveland Browns sent their rookie quarterback, Y.A. Tittle, to the Baltimore Colts. Tittle replaced Bud Schwenk, who signed with the Yankees and took over as starting quarterback for the Colts.

Y.A. went on to score one of the best individual seasons that year from a quarterback. He finished off his rookie season with 2,522 passing yards (third in the league), 16 touchdowns (tied for fourth in the league with Buffalo's George Ratterman), and nine interceptions (the best in the league).

1949

In 1949 the Colts and their fans were hopeful that change for the good would come to the team, but unfortunately for both, the team finished with a 1–11 season.

Y.A. finished the 1949 season with 2,209 passing yards (second in the league) and 14 passing touchdowns (third in the league). But Tittle also threw 18 interceptions, more than any other quarterback in the league.

1950

At the end of the 1949 season, the AAFC merged with the NFL. The Cleveland Browns, the San Francisco 49ers, and the Baltimore Colts were all absorbed into the National Football League.

Tittle's first year in the NFL just didn't stack up to the competition in the new league. Although he passed for 1,884 yards (one of five quarterbacks to do so) he still finished the season 10th in the league with eight passing touchdowns.

With a dismal 1–11 record for the second year in a row, the Colts were disbanded by the NFL.

1951

With the failure of the Baltimore Colts in 1950, the team was sold back to the league and its players became free agents. Tittle was picked up by the San Francisco 49ers and head coach Buck Shaw.

It was one of Y.A.'s least productive seasons because he played behind starter Frankie Albert. All in all Tittle threw for 808 yards, eight touchdowns, and nine interceptions.

1952

The 1952 season handed Tittle more responsibility over his offense, but his completion and touchdown percentages suffered significantly in comparison to his 1951 stats.

Y.A. finished seventh in the league in passing yards (1,407), ninth in touchdowns (11), and second in completion percentage (51 percent). He threw a total of 12 interceptions during the season.

1953

With Frankie Albert now retired, the 1953 season was Tittle's first year as the 49ers' starting quarterback. It turned out to be a great season for both him and the team.

He finished the season fifth in the league in passing yards (2,121), second in the league in touchdowns (20), and second in completion percentage (55.7 percent). 1953 was also the first year that Tittle was elected to play in the Pro Bowl.

1954

1954 was the year of the Million-Dollar Backfield. The 49ers had acquired John Henry Johnson, and together with Tittle, Joe Perry, and Hugh McElhenny they were nearly unstoppable. They finished the season with a 7–4–1 record.

In December 1954 owner Tony Morabito fired Buck Shaw because of his inability to make the championship game and hired assistant coach and scout Red Strader as his replacement.

1954 proved to be a landmark year for the 49ers. Perry became the first player in NFL history to rush for consecutive 1,000-yard seasons, and eight players were sent to the Pro Bowl. On offense were Tittle, Perry, Johnson, Bruno Banducci, and Billy Wilson. On defense were Leo Nomellini, Al Carapella, and Jim Cason.

1954 also proved to be another strong year for Tittle as he remained one of the top quarterbacks in the league. He threw for 2,205 yards (third in the league), had a completion percentage of 57.6 percent (second in the league), threw for nine touchdowns (10th in the league), and threw nine interceptions.

1955

Even with new coach Red Strader, 1955 was a difficult year for both the 49ers and Tittle. Y.A. seemed to be "mistake prone" that year, and despite throwing 17 touchdowns—enough to lead the NFL—his performance suffered in all other categories. His 57 percent completion percentage in 1954 dropped to 51.2 percent in 1955. The nine interceptions he threw in 1954 jumped to 28 in 1955 (leading the league in INTs). The 49ers ended the season with a poor 4–8 record.

1956

After a miserable 1955 season, Red Strader was fired and former star quarterback Frankie Albert became the new head coach. A new rule, the face-mask penalty, became an official penalty for the first time in the NFL. Unfortunately it was only a penalty if it was committed against someone other than the ball carrier.

The misfortune of enduring a second injury-prone season continued into 1956. The 5–6–1 season had a lot to do with Tittle missing more than two full games due to injury. The team suffered greatly when backup quarterback Earl Morrall came onto the field.

Tittle managed to finish the season with 1,641 yards (fourth in the league), a completion percentage of 56.9 percent (second in the league), seven touchdowns (10th in the league), and 12 interceptions.

1957

With Frankie Albert at the helm, the 49ers climbed to a 4–1 record and were alone in first place for the first time in over two years.

On October 27 the 49ers played Chicago at home. At halftime the score was Chicago 17, 49ers 7. Tragically, team owner Tony Morabito suffered a heart attack in the middle of the game and died. The team rallied an emotional second-half comeback and won the game with an 11-yard touchdown pass late in the fourth quarter from Tittle to Billy Wilson.

In their game against the Lions, Tittle threw for over 225 yards in the air and won the game on a fourth-quarter 41-yard throw to first-year player R.C. Owens in what was to become known as the Alley-Oop pass.

1957 proved to be a landmark year for Tittle. For the first time in his career he made it to the postseason playoffs and for the third time he was elected to the Pro Bowl.

His season stats weren't bad either. He threw for 2,157 yards (second in the league), 13 touchdowns (third in the league), and had a career high of 63.1 completion percentage (first in the league)—a number he would never surpass. He threw 15 interceptions.

1958

1958 proved to be an inconsistent year for Tittle. For the first time since 1952 he had to split his position as quarterback with a second-year player, John Brodie out of Stanford.

Y.A. threw for 1,467 yards (second in the league) with a 57.7 percent completion percentage (second in the league). He didn't qualify among the league's leaders in touchdowns.

The 49ers finished the regular season with a 6–6 record.

1959

Frankie Albert resigned as head coach and was replaced by assistant coach Red Hickey. Under Hickey, Tittle gave up more and more playing time to John Brodie. Y.A. ended up suffering one of his worst individual seasons since 1951.

Tittle threw the fewest passes in a season and passed for the fewest yards since 1951. He was eighth in the league for passing yards (1,331), eighth in the league for touchdowns (10), sixth in the league for completion percentage (51.3 percent), and threw a total of 15 interceptions.

Even though his stats had dropped, he was still elected to the Pro Bowl for his fourth appearance.

1960

With the death of league commissioner Bert Bell in the middle of the 1959 season, the league decided to go with an intelligent, young, ambitious man named Pete Rozelle. His incredible accomplishments over the next three decades would change the NFL forever.

Tittle's fate would be different. He lost his starting job at quarterback to John Brodie. He only started four games but impressively won three of the four. His stats were still respectable. He completed 54.3 percent of his passes and threw more touchdowns (four) than interceptions (three) for the first time in a season since 1954. Unfortunately he didn't take enough snaps to qualify in any major category.

1961

1961 found Y.A. traded to the New York Giants.

In need of a future replacement for the aging Charlie Conerly, Giants head coach Allie Sherman brought in veteran All-Pro Y.A. Tittle, who had himself been replaced by a younger quarterback in San Francisco.

1961 proved to be one of the best seasons of Tittle's career. With only 10 starts, Y.A. had a 57.2 percent completion rate, passed for 2,272 yards, and threw for 17 touchdowns and only 12 interceptions. This was his highest touchdown total since the 20 touchdowns he threw in 1953 and the most passing yards that he had ever thrown in the NFL. He also threw the fewest number of interceptions since 1956. The Giants finished the season 10–4–1.

But for Tittle, the most important part of the '61 season was making it to the championship game, a first in his career.

1962

The expectations for the Giants were high going into the 1962 season. Charlie Conerly had retired, and Y.A. was the starter for the team.

The Giants' regular-season record was 11–3, and they found themselves playing the Green Bay Packers again for a second consecutive championship game.

1962 turned out to be Tittle's best year in the NFL. His season completion rate was 53.3 percent, he passed for 3,324 yards, and he threw 33 touchdowns and 20 interceptions. He also threw for 700 more yards than he had thrown in his entire career and 1,000 more yards than he had ever thrown in the NFL.

1963

Thanks to commissioner Pete Rozelle, the 1963 season saw the NFL benefitting from the league's expansion and increased network contracts.

Coming off of a second straight championship appearance, the Giants were ready for another strong season. They finished the year with an 11–3 regular-season record and were on their way to a third consecutive championship game—but this time it was against the Chicago Bears.

Tittle's stats were much improved. He threw for 3,145 yards, completed 60.2 percent of his passes, and threw 36 touchdowns and 14 interceptions. His 36 touchdown passes were an NFL record for that time. He was elected to his seventh Pro Bowl appearance, his third straight with the Giants.

1964

Having been to three straight championship games, no one was ready for what would happen to the Giants in 1964. They would post a miserable 2–10–2 record for the season.

While 1963 may have been one of Y.A.'s best seasons, 1964 was one of his worst. He threw for under 2,000 yards and only 10 touchdowns. His 22 interceptions were more than double his touchdown total, and the ineffectiveness of Tittle and the rest of the Giants team became the reason for their collapse. After a long talk during the off-season with teammate and good friend Frank Gifford, Tittle and Gifford both decided to retire from professional football.

APPENDIX II
Team Schedules

- Baltimore Colts 1948–1950

- San Francisco 49ers 1951–1960

- New York Giants 1961–1964

1948 Baltimore Colts Team Schedule

Week	Date	Opponent	Score	Win/Loss	Record
1	Sept 5	New York Yankees	45–28	Won	1–0
2	Sept 10	@Chicago Rockets	14–21	Lost	1–1
3	Sept 16	@New York Yankees	27–14	Won	2–1
4	Sept 26	Brooklyn Dodgers	35–20	Won	3–1
5	Oct 5	Cleveland Browns	10–14	Lost	3–2
6	Oct 10	San Francisco 49ers	14–56	Lost	3–3
7	Oct 15	@Los Angeles Dons	29–14	Won	4–3
8	Oct 24	@San Francisco 49ers	10–21	Lost	4–4
9	Oct 31	@Buffalo Bills	17–35	Lost	4–5
10	Nov 7	@Cleveland Browns	7–28	Lost	4–6
11	Nov 14	Chicago Rockets	38–24	Won	5–6
12	Nov 21	Los Angeles Dons	14–17	Lost	5–7
13	Nov 28	@Brooklyn Dodgers	38–20	Won	6–7
14	Dec 5	Buffalo Bills	35–15	Won	7–7
Champ	Dec 12	Buffalo Bills	17–28	Lost	7–8

1949 Baltimore Colts Team Schedule

Week	Date	Opponent	Score	Win/Loss	Record
1	Aug 28	@San Francisco 49ers	17–31	Lost	0–1
2	Sept 2	@Los Angeles Dons	17–49	Lost	0–2
3	Sept 11	@Cleveland Browns	0–21	Lost	0–3
4	Sept 16	@Chicago Hornets	7–35	Lost	0–4
5	Sept 25	Cleveland Browns	20–28	Lost	0–5
6	Oct 2	@Buffalo Bills	35–28	Won	1–5
7	Oct 16	New York Yankees	21–24	Lost	1–6
8	Oct 23	Chicago Hornets	7–17	Lost	1–7
9	Oct 30	@New York Yankees	14–21	Lost	1–8
10	Nov 6	San Francisco 49ers	10–28	Lost	1–9
11	Nov 20	Los Angeles Dons	10–21	Lost	1–10
12	Nov 27	Buffalo Bills	14–38	Lost	1–11

1950 Baltimore Colts Team Schedule

Week	Date	Opponent	Score	Win/Loss	Record
1	Sept 17	Washington Redskins	14–38	Lost	0–1
2	Sept 24	Cleveland Browns	0–31	Lost	0–2
3	Oct 2	@Chicago Cardinals	13–55	Lost	0–3
4	Oct 15	Philadelphia Eagles	14–24	Lost	0–4
5	Oct 22	@Los Angeles Rams	27–70	Lost	0–5
6	Oct 29	@San Francisco 49ers	14–17	Lost	0–6
7	Nov 5	Green Bay Packers	41–21	Won	1–6
8	Nov 12	@Pittsburgh Steelers	7–17	Lost	1–7
9	Nov 19	New York Giants	20–55	Lost	1–8
10	Nov 26	@Washington Redskins	28–38	Lost	1–9
11	Dec 3	Detroit Lions	21–45	Lost	1–10
12	Dec 10	@New York Yankees	14–51	Lost	1–11

1951 San Francisco 49ers Team Schedule

Week	Date	Opponent	Score	Win/Loss	Record
1	Sep 30	Cleveland Browns	24–10	Won	1–0
2	Oct 6	@Philadelphia Eagles	14–21	Lost	1–1
3	Oct 14	@Pittsburgh Steelers	28–24	Won	2–1
4	Oct 21	@Chicago Bears	7–13	Lost	2–2
5	Oct 28	Los Angeles Rams	44–17	Won	3–2
6	Nov 4	@Los Angeles Rams	16–23	Lost	3–3
7	Nov 11	New York Yankees	19–14	Won	4–3
8	Nov 18	Chicago Cardinals	21–27	Lost	4–4
9	Nov 25	@New York Yankees	10–10	Tie	4–4–1
10	Dec 2	@Detroit Lions	20–10	Won	5–4–1
11	Dec 9	Green Bay Packers	31–19	Won	6–4–1
12	Dec 16	Detroit Lions	21–17	Won	7–4–1

1952 San Francisco 49ers Team Schedule

Week	Date	Opponent	Score	Win/Loss	Record
1	Sept 28	Detroit Lions	17–13	Won	1–0
2	Oct 5	@Dallas Texans	37–14	Won	2–0
3	Oct 12	@Detroit Lions	38–0	Won	3–0
4	Oct 19	@Chicago Bears	40–16	Won	4–0
5	Oct 26	Dallas Texans	48–21	Won	5–0
6	Nov 2	Chicago Bears	17–20	Lost	5–1
7	Nov 9	@New York Giants	14–23	Lost	5–2
8	Nov 16	@Washington Redskins	23–17	Won	6–2
9	Nov 23	@Los Angeles Rams	9–35	Lost	6–3
10	Nov 30	Los Angeles Rams	21–34	Lost	6–4
11	Dec 7	Pittsburgh Steelers	7–24	Lost	6–5
12	Dec 14	Green Bay Packers	24–14	Won	7–5

1953 San Francisco 49ers Team Schedule

Week	Date	Opponent	Score	Win/Loss	Record
1	Sept 27	Philadelphia Eagles	31–21	Won	1–0
2	Oct 4	Los Angeles Rams	31–30	Won	2–0
3	Oct 11	@Detroit Lions	21–24	Lost	2–1
4	Oct 18	@Chicago Bears	35–28	Won	3–1
5	Oct 25	Detroit Lions	10–14	Lost	3–2
6	Nov 1	Chicago Bears	24–14	Won	4–2
7	Nov 8	@Los Angeles Rams	31–27	Won	5–2
8	Nov 15	@Cleveland Browns	21–23	Lost	5–3
9	Nov 22	@Green Bay Packers	37–7	Won	6–3
10	Nov 29	@Baltimore Colts	38–21	Won	7–3
11	Dec 6	Green Bay Packers	48–14	Won	8–3
12	Dec 13	Baltimore Colts	45–14	Won	9–3

1954 San Francisco 49ers Team Schedule

Week	Date	Opponent	Score	Win/Loss	Record
1	Sept 26	Washington Redskins	41–7	Won	1–0
2	Oct 3	@Los Angeles Rams	24–24	Tie	1–0–1
3	Oct 10	@Green Bay Packers	23–17	Won	2–0–1
4	Oct 17	@Chicago Bears	31–24	Won	3–0–1
5	Oct 24	Detroit Lions	37–31	Won	4–0–1
6	Oct 31	Chicago Bears	27–31	Lost	4–1–1
7	Nov 7	Los Angeles Rams	34–42	Lost	4–2–1
8	Nov 14	@Detroit Lions	7–48	Lost	4–3–1
9	Nov 20	@Pittsburgh Steelers	31–3	Won	5–3–1
10	Nov 28	@Baltimore Colts	13–17	Lost	5–4–1
11	Dec 5	Green Bay Packers	35–0	Won	6–4–1
12	Dec 11	Baltimore Colts	10–7	Won	7–4–1

1955 San Francisco 49ers Team Schedule

Week	Date	Opponent	Score	Win/Loss	Record
1	Sept 25	Los Angeles Rams	14–23	Lost	0–1
2	Oct 2	Cleveland Browns	3–38	Lost	0–2
3	Oct 9	@Chicago Bears	20–19	Won	1–2
4	Oct 16	@Detroit Lions	27–24	Won	2–2
5	Oct 23	Chicago Bears	23–34	Lost	2–3
6	Oct 30	Detroit Lions	38–21	Won	3–3
7	Nov 6	@Los Angeles Rams	14–27	Lost	3–4
8	Nov 13	@Washington Redskins	0–7	Lost	3–5
9	Nov 20	@Green Bay Packers	21–27	Lost	3–6
10	Nov 27	@Baltimore Colts	14–26	Lost	3–7
11	Dec 4	Green Bay Packers	7–28	Lost	3–8
12	Dec 11	Baltimore Colts	35–24	Won	4–8

1956 San Francisco 49ers Team Schedule

Week	Date	Opponent	Score	Win/Loss	Record
1	Sept 30	New York Giants	21–38	Lost	0–1
2	Oct 7	Los Angeles Rams	33–30	Won	1–1
3	Oct 14	@Chicago Bears	7–31	Lost	1–2
4	Oct 21	@Detroit Lions	17–20	Lost	1–3
5	Oct 28	Chicago Bears	21–38	Lost	1–4
6	Nov 4	Detroit Lions	13–17	Lost	1–5
7	Nov 11	@Los Angeles Rams	6–30	Lost	1–6
8	Nov 18	@Green Bay Packers	17–16	Won	2–6
9	Nov 25	@Philadelphia Eagles	10–10	Tie	2–6–1
10	Dec 2	@Baltimore Colts	20–17	Won	3–6–1
11	Dec 8	Green Bay Packers	38–20	Won	4–6–1
12	Dec 16	Baltimore Colts	30–17	Won	5–6–1

1957 San Francisco 49ers Team Schedule

Week	Date	Opponent	Score	Win/Loss	Record
1	Sept 29	Chicago Cardinals	10–20	Lost	0–1
2	Oct 6	Los Angeles Rams	23–20	Won	1–1
3	Oct 13	@Chicago Bears	21–17	Won	2–1
4	Oct 20	@Green Bay Packers	24–14	Won	3–1
5	Oct 27	Chicago Bears	21–17	Won	4–1
6	Nov 3	Detroit Lions	35–31	Won	5–1
7	Nov 10	@Los Angeles Rams	24–37	Lost	5–2
8	Nov 17	@Detroit Liions	10–31	Lost	5–3
9	Nov 24	@Baltimore Colts	21–27	Lost	5–4
10	Dec 1	@New York Giants	27–17	Won	6–4
11	Dec 8	Baltimore Colts	17–13	Won	7–4
12	Dec 15	Green Bay Packers	27–20	Won	8–4
Playoffs	Dec 22	Detroit Lions	27–31	Lost	8–5

1958 San Francisco 49ers Team Schedule

Week	Date	Opponent	Score	Win/Loss	Record
1	Sept 28	Pittsburgh Steelers	23–20	Won	1–0
2	Oct 5	Los Angeles Rams	3–33	Lost	1–1
3	Oct 12	@Chicago Bears	6–28	Lost	1–2
4	Oct 19	@Philadelphia Eagles	30–24	Won	2–2
5	Oct 26	Chicago Bears	14–27	Lost	2–3
6	Nov 2	Detroit Lions	24–21	Won	3–3
7	Nov 9	@Los Angeles Rams	7–56	Lost	3–4
8	Nov 16	@Detroit Lions	21–35	Lost	3–5
9	Nov 23	@Green Bay Packers	33–12	Won	4–5
10	Nov 30	@Baltimore Colts	27–35	Lost	4–6
11	Dec 7	Green Bay Packers	48–21	Won	5–6
12	Dec 14	Baltimore Colts	21–12	Won	6–6

1959 San Francisco 49ers Team Schedule

Week	Date	Opponent	Score	Win/Loss	Record
1	Sept 27	Philadelphia Eagles	24–14	Won	1–0
2	Oct 4	Los Angeles Rams	34–0	Won	2–0
3	Oct 11	@Green Bay Packers	20–21	Lost	2–1
4	Oct 18	@Detroit Lions	34–13	Won	3–1
5	Oct 25	Chicago Bears	20–17	Won	4–1
6	Nov 1	Detroit Lions	33–7	Won	5–1
7	Nov 8	@Los Angeles Rams	24–16	Won	6–1
8	Nov 15	@Chicago Bears	3–14	Lost	6–2
9	Nov 22	@Baltimore Colts	14–45	Lost	6–3
10	Nov 29	@Cleveland Browns	21–20	Won	7–3
11	Dec 5	Baltimore Colts	14–34	Lost	7–4
12	Dec 13	Green Bay Packers	14–36	Lost	7–5

1960 San Francisco 49ers Team Schedule

Week	Date	Opponent	Score	Win/Loss	Record
1	Sept 25	New York Giants	19–21	Lost	0–1
2	Oct 2	Los Angeles Rams	13–9	Won	1–1
3	Oct 9	@Detroit Lions	14–10	Won	2–1
4	Oct 16	@Chicago Bears	10–27	Lost	2–2
5	Oct 23	@Green Bay Packers	14–41	Lost	2–3
6	Oct 30	Chicago Bears	25–7	Won	3–3
7	Nov 6	Detroit Lions	0–24	Lost	3–4
8	Nov 20	@Dallas Cowboys	26–14	Won	4–4
9	Nov 27	@Baltimore Colts	30–22	Won	5–4
10	Dec 4	@Los Angeles Rams	23–7	Won	6–4
11	Dec 10	Green Bay Packers	0–13	Lost	6–5
12	Dec 18	Baltimore Colts	34–10	Won	7–5

1961 New York Giants Team Schedule

Week	Date	Opponent	Score	Win/Loss	Record
1	Sept 17	St. Louis Cardinals	10–21	Lost	0–1
2	Sept 24	@Pittsburgh Steelers	17–14	Won	1–1
3	Oct 1	@Washington Redskins	24–21	Won	2–1
4	Oct 8	@St. Louis Cardinals	24–9	Won	3–1
5	Oct 15	@Dallas Cowboys	31–10	Won	4–1
6	Oct 22	Los Angeles Rams	24–14	Won	5–1
7	Oct 29	Dallas Cowboys	16–17	Lost	5–2
8	Nov 5	Washington Redskins	53–0	Won	6–2
9	Nov 12	Philadelphia Eagles	38–21	Won	7–2
10	Nov 19	Pittsburgh Steelers	42–21	Won	8–2
11	Nov 26	@Cleveland Browns	37–21	Won	9–2
12	Dec 3	@Green Bay Packers	17–20	Lost	9–3
13	Dec 10	@Philadelphia Eagles	28–24	Won	10–3
14	Dec 17	Cleveland Browns	7–7	Tie	10–3–1
Playoffs	Dec 31	Green Bay Packers	0–37	Lost	10–4–1

1962 New York Giants Team Schedule

Week	Date	Opponent	Score	Win/Loss	Record
1	Sept 16	@Cleveland Browns	7–17	Lost	0–1
2	Sept 23	@Philadelphia Eagles	29–13	Won	1–1
3	Sept 30	@Pittsburgh Steelers	31–27	Won	2–1
4	Oct 7	@St. Louis Cardinals	31–14	Won	3–1
5	Oct 14	Pittsburgh Steelers	17–20	Lost	3–2
6	Oct 21	Detroit Lions	17–14	Won	4–2
7	Oct 28	Washington Redskins	34–49	Won	5–2
8	Nov 4	St. Louis Cardinals	31–28	Won	6–2
9	Nov 11	@Dallas Cowboys	41–10	Won	7–2
10	Nov 18	Philadelphia Eagles	19–14	Won	8–2
11	Nov 25	@Washington Redskins	42–24	Won	9–2
12	Dec 2	@Chicago Bears	26–24	Won	10–2
13	Dec 9	Cleveland Browns	17–13	Won	11–2
14	Dec 16	Dallas Cowboys	41–31	Won	12–2
Playoffs	Dec 30	Green Bay Packers	7–16	Lost	12–3

1963 New York Giants Team Schedule

Week	Date	Opponent	Score	Win/Loss	Record
1	Sept 15	@Baltimore Colts	37–28	Won	1–0
2	Sept 22	@Pittsburgh Steelers	0–31	Lost	1–1
3	Sept 29	@Philadelphia Eagles	37–14	Won	2–1
4	Oct 6	@Washington Redskins	24–14	Won	3–1
5	Oct 13	Cleveland Browns	24–35	Lost	3–2
6	Oct 20	Dallas Cowboys	37–21	Won	4–2
7	Oct 27	@Cleveland Browns	33–6	Won	5–2
8	Nov 3	@St. Louis Cardinals	38–21	Won	6–2
9	Nov 10	Philadelphia Eagles	42–14	Won	7–2
10	Nov 17	San Francisco 49ers	48–14	Won	8–2
11	Nov 24	St. Louis Cardinals	17–24	Lost	8–3
12	Dec 1	@Dallas Cowboys	34–27	Won	9–3
13	Dec 8	Washington Redskins	44–14	Won	10–3
14	Dec 15	Pittsburgh Steelers	33–17	Won	11–3
Playoffs	Dec 29	@Chicago Bears	10–14	Lost	11–4

1964 New York Giants Team Schedule

Week	Date	Opponent	Score	Win/Loss	Record
1	Sept 13	@Philadelphia Eagles	7–38	Lost	0–1
2	Sept 20	@Pittsburgh Steelers	24–27	Lost	0–2
3	Sept 25	Washington Redskins	13–10	Won	1–2
4	Oct 4	@Detroit Lions	3–26	Lost	1–3
5	Oct 11	@Dallas Cowboys	13–13	Tie	1–3–1
6	Oct 18	Philadelphia Eagles	17–23	Lost	1–4–1
7	Oct 25	@Cleveland Browns	20–42	Lost	1–5–1
8	Nov 1	St. Louis Cardinals	34–17	Won	2–5–1
9	Nov 8	Dallas Cowboys	21–31	Lost	2–6–1
10	Nov 15	@St. Louis Cardinals	10–10	Tie	2–6–2
11	Nov 22	Pittsburgh Steelers	17–44	Lost	2–7–2
12	Nov 29	@Washington Redskins	21–36	Lost	2–8–2
13	Dec 6	Minnesota Vikings	21–30	Lost	2–9–2
14	Dec 12	Cleveland Browns	20–52	Lost	2–10–2

APPENDIX III
Passing Statistics

Year	Tm	G	GS	Cmp	Att	Cmp%	Yds	TD	Int	Lng	Y/G	Rate
1948	BCL	14	12	161	289	55.7	2522	16	9	80	180.1	90.3
1949	BCL	11	7	148	289	51.2	2209	14	18	80	200.8	66.8
1950	BAL	12	9	161	315	51.1	1884	8	19	62	157.0	52.9
1951	SFO	12	1	63	114	55.3	808	8	9	48	67.3	68.2
1952	SFO	12	5	106	208	51.0	1407	11	12	77	117.3	66.3
1953	SFO	11	10	149	259	57.5	2121	20	16	71	192.8	84.1
1954	SFO	12	11	170	295	57.6	2205	9	9	70	183.8	78.7
1955	SFO	12	12	147	287	51.2	2185	17	28	78	182.1	56.6
1956	SFO	10	8	124	218	56.9	1641	7	12	77	164.1	68.6
1957	SFO	12	11	176	279	63.1	2157	13	15	46	179.8	80.0
1958	SFO	11	6	120	208	57.7	1467	9	15	64	133.4	63.9
1959	SFO	11	10	102	199	51.3	1331	10	15	75	121.0	58.0
1960	SFO	9	4	69	127	54.3	694	4	3	45	77.1	70.8
1961	NYG	13	10	163	285	57.2	2272	17	12	62	174.8	85.3
1962	NYG	14	14	200	375	53.3	3224	33	20	69	230.3	89.5
1963	NYG	13	13	221	367	60.2	3145	36	14	70	241.9	104.8
1964	NYG	14	11	147	281	52.3	1798	10	22	54	128.4	51.6
Career		203	154	2427	4395	55.2	33070	242	248	80	162.9	74.3

Sources

Ballay, Chris. "Sounds from the Past: Tittle Only Tiger to Be Selected Twice in Top 10 of the Draft." http://media.www.lsureveille.com/media/storage/paper868/news/2007/05/01/Sports/Sounds.From.The.Past-2889657.shtml (accessed May 28, 2008).

Bay Area Sports Hall of Fame. "Y.A. Tittle." http://www.bashof.org/inducteebios/yatittle.htm (accessed August 2, 2008).

Cavanaugh, Jack. *Giants Among Men: How Robustelli, Huff, Gifford and the Giants Made New York a Football Town and Changed the NFL.* New York: Random House, 2008.

Croker, Garrett. How They Scored. www.howtheyscored.com (accessed October 23, 2008).

Crowe, Jerome. "It Turned Out to Be the Biggest Snap of His Career." http://articles.latimes.com/2008/jan/28/sports/sp-crowe28 (accessed May 28, 2008).

Dickey, Glenn. *San Francisco 49ers: The First Fifty Years.* Atlanta: Turner Publishing, Inc., 1995.

Fucillo, David. 49ers Year-by-Year. http://www.ninersnation.com/section/49ers-year-by-year (accessed October 23, 2008).

Gifford, Frank and Harry Waters. *The Whole Ten Yards.* New York: Random House, 1993.

Hardesty, Dan. *The Louisiana Tigers: LSU Football.* Huntsville, AL: The Strode Publishers, 1975.

Hession, Joseph. *Forty Niners: Looking Back*. San Francisco: Foghorn Press, 1985.

———. "Hugh McElhenny: The King." The Coffin Corner (Vol. 8, No. 4 (1986)). www.profootballresearchers.org/Coffin_Corner/08-04-264. pdf (accessed July 9, 2008).

Howler, George. "Fame Didn't Pass Tittle—Quarterback Looks Back on 'Lucky' Career." *The Santa Rosa Press Democrat*, January 27, 1991, Profiles section.

Jacobs, Martin S. *Before They Were Champions: The San Francisco 49ers' 1958 Season*. San Francisco: Martin Jacobs, 2002.

New York Daily News. *New York Giants: 75 Years of Football Memories from the Archives of the New York Daily News*. Champaign, IL: Sports Publishing LLC, 1999.

Newhouse, Dave. *The Million Dollar Backfield: The San Francisco 49ers in the 1950s*. Berkeley, CA: Frog, Ltd./North Atlantic Books, 2000.

Pro Football Hall of Fame. "Y.A. Tittle." http://www.profootballhof. com/hof/member.jsp?player_id=214 (accessed May 3, 2008).

Pro Football Reference, www.pro-football-reference.com (accessed July 9, 2008).

Pro Football Reference. "Y.A. Tittle." http://www.pro-football-reference .com/players/T/TittY.00.htm (accessed June 1, 2008).

Rand, Jonathan. *Riddell Presents the Gridiron's Greatest Quarterbacks*. Champaign, IL: Sports Publishing LLC, 2004.

Sabol, Steve. NFL Films Presents: *Y.A. Tittle, NFL Scrapbook*. NFL Films. June 1996.

San Francisco 49ers Historical Moments. http://www.sportsecyclopedia .com/nfl/sf49/49ers.html (accessed October 5, 2008).

Siegel, Robert. "A Football Giant and His Hero-Worshipping Daughter." http://www.npr.org/templates/story/story.php?storyId=6098928 (accessed May 28, 2008).

Sports Illustrated Vault. "49ers Quarterback Y.A. Tittle." http://vault. sportsillustrated.cnn.com/vault/article/magazine/MAG1008654/ index.htm (accessed August 1, 2008).

Tittle, Y.A.and Don Smith. *Y.A. Tittle: I Pass! My Story as Told to Don Smith*. New York: Franklin Watts, Inc., 1964.

Tittle-De Laet, Dianne. *Giants and Heroes: A Daughter's Memories of Y.A. Tittle*. South Royalton, VT: Steerforth Press, 1995.

Whittingham, Richard (ed.). *The Fireside Book of Pro Football: An Anthology of the Best, Most Entertaining Writing about Professional Football*. New York: Simon and Schuster, 1989.

Y.A. Tittle's official website, http://www.yatittle.net.

About the Authors

Y.A. TITTLE PLAYED HIGH SCHOOL FOOTBALL in Marshall, Texas, and then left to play for the Louisiana State Tigers. His extraordinary passing ability inspired LSU coach Bernie Moore to abandon the single wing for the T formation. The Cleveland Browns of the All-America Football Conference were impressed with what they saw in Tittle  and drafted him in 1948. He played two seasons with the Baltimore Colts of the All-America Football Conference after being traded by the Browns and played one season with the Colts in the National Football League.

With the failure of the Baltimore Colts in 1950, the team was sold back to the league, and their players became free agents. Tittle was picked up by the San Francisco 49ers and head coach Buck Shaw. He played 10 seasons with the San Francisco 49ers and a final four seasons with the New York Giants.

Although Tittle had excellent personal statistics while playing for the Colts and 49ers, the one thing that eluded him was a championship. Then, in 1961, when Tittle was traded to New York, it looked like his fate would change. The Giants were contenders. However, when he joined the team, he was about as welcome as the plague. The Giants were a veteran, close-knit group, proud of their past successes. They knew that Tittle would be battling a team favorite, 40-year-old Charlie Conerly, for the quarterback job.

When the 1961 season started, Tittle and Conerly shared the quarterbacking duties, but as the Giants moved nearer to the NFL Eastern Division crown, it became more and more evident that Tittle was the guy making it all possible. That same year Y.A. was named the NFL's Most Valuable Player.

In 1962 Tittle played even better, with 33 touchdown passes and a career-high 3,224 yards. A year later, his touchdown stats went up to 36, he completed 60.2% of his passes, and again he was named NFL Player of the Year. A terrific competitor who was always willing to play while hurt, Tittle led the Giants to divisional titles in 1961, 1962, and 1963. Even though they failed to win the coveted NFL crown, the years when Tittle was at the helm were truly the Giants' glory years.

UNIVERSITY OF SAN FRANCISCO GRADUATE and author **Dr. Kristine Setting Clark** is a feature writer for the San Francisco 49ers' and Dallas Cowboys' *Gameday* magazine. She has authored or coauthored numerous books, including *Legends of the Hall: The Fabulous Fifties*; *Undefeated, Untied, and Uninvited*; *St Clair: I'll Take It Raw!*; and *A Cowboy's Life*, about Hall of Fame member Bob Lilly. This year she will be working on a book with Jim Taylor of the Green Bay Packers.

In 1977 Kristine was diagnosed with Stage IV Hodgkin's Disease and was given three months to live. She eventually beat the disease after enduring 10 months of blindness caused by the grueling chemotherapy treatments. She is in the process of writing her memoir, *Don't Call Me Courageous!*, and the television treatment has been written by Jamie Williams, former San Francisco 49ers tight end and screenwriter of the movie *Any Given Sunday*.

Dr. Clark resides in Northern California with her husband and has two grown children and a grandson. Her grandson, Justin, is the godson of Hall of Fame member Bob St. Clair.

Memories of my daughter is not enough -- not even close. The hurt doesn't go away. Faith gives me peace of mind. The hurt goes on a shelf.